A YEAR OF JOURNALING THROUGH GRIEF

DR. SHEILA COOPERMAN

This work depicts actual events in the life of the author as truthfully as recollection permits. Some names and identifying characteristics have been changed to protect the privacy of individuals.

Copyright © 2025 by Sheila Cooperman

All rights reserved

First edition, 2025

Cover and book design by Spring Cedars

ISBN 978-1-963117-59-2 (paperback)
ISBN 978-1-963117-60-8 (hardback)
ISBN 978-1-963117-61-5 (ebook)

Published by Spring Cedars
Denver, Colorado
www.springcedars.com

*This book is lovingly dedicated to
my mother, Julia Schwartz, who passed away on December 29, 1969,
and to my mother, Trudy Schwartz, who left us on March 25, 1998.
In addition, this book is dedicated to my canine best friend, Tucker,
who crossed the Rainbow Bridge on August 11, 2023.
All these loves taught me about life, loss, and living each day to the fullest.
I am who I am because of you all.
You live forever in my heart.*

CONTENTS

FOREWORD	i
WEEK 1	1
WEEK 2	7
WEEK 3	10
WEEK 3.5	14
WEEK 4	15
WEEK 5	20
WEEK 6	28
WEEK 7	40
WEEK 8	49
WEEK 9	60
WEEK 10	66
WEEK 11	75
WEEK 12	81
WEEK 13	94
WEEK 14	98
WEEK 15	102
WEEK 16	107
WEEK 17	114

WEEK 18	121
WEEK 19	129
WEEK 20	136
WEEK 21	143
WEEK 22	147
WEEK 23	157
WEEK 24	164
WEEK 25	167
WEEK 26	171
WEEK 27	174
WEEK 28	180
WEEK 29	184
WEEK 30	189
WEEK 31	194
WEEK 32	199
WEEK 33	204
WEEK 34	208
WEEK 35	211
WEEK 36	215
WEEK 37	218
WEEK 38	221
WEEK 39	228
WEEK 40	233
WEEK 41	236
WEEK 42	240

WEEK 43	243
WEEK 44	247
WEEK 45	251
WEEK 46	255
WEEK 47	259
WEEK 48	262
WEEK 49	266
WEEK 50	270
WEEK 51	274
WEEK 52	277
EPILOGUE	281
ABOUT THE AUTHOR	285

FOREWORD

Can I remember the beginning?

My husband, David, has always been a dog owner. He had three dogs before we had Tucker and lost three dogs before our Tucker was taken from us. Many years passed between the death of his last dog, Jake, and Tucker coming into our lives. David and I were living alone. Our collective children are grown and have lives of their own. I was a full-time schoolteacher, left early in the morning, and rarely returned before four in the afternoon. As a teacher, I was surrounded all day by noise and humanity. Screaming kids, dozens of teachers, countless phone calls, bells, and whistles. Middle school. Controlled chaos. The school environment was a good match for me. I had the stimulus and social interaction I needed and craved, but David needed something else. David worked at home alone. His only company was the quiet and himself. David is more comfortable with solitude than I am, and he does not feel the consistent need to do something. So, when he said he wanted a dog. I said, "OK." He was home all day, and I was not. If a dog was going to keep him company and keep him happy, why would I possibly object? It was, after all, going to be his dog. His charge. His responsibility.

But what kind of dog? He had always had very large dogs. He had an affinity for Bernese Mountain Dogs. I was more inclined to have a smaller dog.

Not one of those yappy, put-in-a-bag-and-take-to-Bloomingdale's dogs, rather a smaller dog that was more manageable,. But when push came to shove, I did not care because, remember, I was pretty much a bystander and an observer in this canine experiment.

David, because we live in the digital age, took several online surveys. You know, the ones that say, "Find the Dog That Was Meant for You." Or "Get Matched," a dating site for humans and dogs. Well, no matter what survey he took, he kept getting matched with a breed he and I had never heard of. The Boykin Spaniel. And again, my indifference played into the decision. I thought, if that is what you want, David, if that is the dog you are going to research, my blessings to you.

So, he did some research and chose the dog. We found a reputable breeder—I knew nothing about rescues—and we picked up our swamp poodle (a nickname I didn't even know existed). After taking the long ferry trip across the Long Island Sound in Connecticut to Long Island, we drove to a small town somewhere out on one of the forks to pick up our new, his new, dog. What a tiny little ball of brown fur. I will admit he was cute as he sat on my lap on the way home. Then he promptly threw up.

We got him home, and we were introduced to puppyhood. David took charge of most of his training. Housebreaking and crate training. His nighttime whimpers did not bother me as he got used to his crate. And that is something that, when I look back on, surprises me, especially since as time went by, I would do (and did) anything to make him happy and would have traveled anywhere to treat him when he got sick if it would have helped.

His cuteness began to grow on me. His tiny little brown body lying on the couch, resting in the sun. His tiny Boykin sprawl. He had this cute attachment to small plastic water bottles that he would toss around in a little section of the yard we created for him. And his little squeal of delight as his puppy legs would carry him across the pool to grab the ball—the beginning of his love affair with blue racquetballs. And his big eyes and big pink tongue and big paws and big heart that captured me completely.

As my attachment to Tucker grew, it was almost as though our circadian rhythms matched. I came to know exactly when something was not right. His appetite was off by an ounce, or he shook his head one too many times, or he didn't seem as spry. And sure enough, when I took him to the vet because I needed to, even if David thought it might be a little premature, I was right. I was his person, and there was nothing he did that I did not love.

I don't know when the shift occurred. I can't pinpoint it, but suddenly, I realized how important Tucker was to me—to us. He was a member of the family, to be considered as important as any other family member. We planned around him. I especially became very cognizant of the amount of time we spent away from him. I realized that I was anthropomorphizing the dog, treating him as though he were as human as you or me. I would ask countless questions. "Does he know I am gone? Does he think I am not coming back? What do you think he is doing?" "Is he mad at me for leaving?" And I really wanted to know. I did not want him to be mad at me. I did not want to create any emotional damage. And thus began a relationship that David sometimes said was "bordering on the unnatural."

In many ways, Tucker became integrated into my everyday life when I was not at home. My students, from the first day of school, knew that "Tucker was the best dog in the world." The password to enter the classroom: "Tucker is the best dog on the planet." I taught grammar using Tucker as the subject of the sentence. I created a pet page on our classroom website; Tucker was the main page. I handed out Boykin Spaniel coloring pages when the students needed something to do during their free time. Everyone knew about Tucker. Everyone knew how I felt. When I would ridiculously ask David, "How much do you love Tucker?" he would always respond, "Not as much as you do." I think he was right.

I have a good friend who told me after reading one of my posts that she had never seen anyone who had such a deep love for a dog. Her name is Allison. It is important for me to explain what I mean by "posts." Much of my early writing was posted each week (and still is) on a series of grief pages on Facebook. Allison, I believe you are right.

So, this is at the heart of my grief. A love and a bond that I was not ready to give up. A love and a bond that I did not know was as strong as it was. Joni Mitchell had it right in her 1970s song, *Big Yellow Taxi*: "Don't it always seem to go that you don't know what you got till it's gone." Except I did know.

August 12, 2023

I lost him. I lost my special boy last night. We released him from his pain. Tucker fought hard for eight weeks. His lungs succumbed to metastatic disease. He had his last swim yesterday and held onto his ball. My Nubby-Bean was my everything. He made me laugh, and yesterday, he made me cry. Run free, my boy. Chase the balls. Dive in the pool. I have adored you for your whole life, and I am going to miss you for the rest of mine. Save a seat for me in the chair, Bean. I'll see you on the other side. You took my heart away.

WEEK 1

It is a long, winding post like a long and winding road. It is a stream of consciousness. It will be one week tonight that I lost my best boy. Do not feel obligated to read this. I miss him.

The anticipatory grief was painful. Not more painful than his actual passing, but a different type of painful. The vigilance that was required was done out of love, but part of the struggle was the sense of futility. His death was imminent, yet I could understand how one can live in the world of hope and denial.

Elisabeth Kübler-Ross was right. He is not sick. He will be fine. He will be the miracle dog, the dog that makes it, the dog that proves all the researchers wrong. So what? He has a mutated B-cell lymphoma. So what? That mutation might just be the one that responds so well to all the treatments that his remission can be measured in years, not months or weeks. I started cooking the Canine Cancer diet for him. I researched the supplements. What did I think? That it was going to cure canine lymphoma? That it was going to extend his life? Maybe—but it made me feel that I was doing something to control my anxiety over what was happening. The lack of control, the unfairness of it all, the inability to fix it.

He responded to nothing. Yet, with each new treatment, I

watched, and journaled, and waited. Observing every move he made, his bowels, his sleeping, his activity, his eating. My heart skipped a beat or 10,000 every time he didn't drink, every time he turned down food, every time he moved. His behavior changed. He could not settle himself on the pillow he usually slept on next to my head. He jumped off the bed and settled on the floor. Why? He always slept on the bed. Was it because he was hot due to the drugs? Was the tile floor cooler? Or was he withdrawing because he instinctively knew his end was nearing and he was separating from his pack—from us?

When you live in the world of anticipatory grief, your mind is hard to control. Is he in pain? Or is it me who is in pain? I looked for signs of hope. I analyzed everything. He was not an unhappy dog, from the looks of it. I tried so hard to take pleasure in that, but I did not do so well in the live-in-the-moment world.

I still threw the ball. I still went outside with him anytime he wanted. He did not know he was sick, but I did, and that was painful. The "when will it happen," the fear of watching him deteriorate, the loss. I found myself feeling that grief is torture. Grieving about when it is going to happen and then grieving when it does.

There is a sense of relief that comes with his passing. He is not suffering, and I am not suffering in the way I was. The medication routine, the vigilance in caring for him, which was really miracle-searching. It was bargaining. If I give him this medication or this food or that supplement, he will be okay. He will be fine. He will be my Tucker for a long time. What do you mean it won't work? How dare you tell me that you are going to rip a piece of my heart out.

In the Broadway show *Hamilton*, Hamilton loses his son who was shot in a gun duel. Hamilton is understandably distressed and sings that "it's quiet uptown" after his son dies. I feel that silence. It is quiet here. The pool gurgles, but my Bean is not running around its edges, trying to time the exact moment and location to jump in to retrieve the ball in one shot. He is not standing on the edge surveying where the frogs might be. He is not whining to swim with his ball in his mouth. It is just a pool of water. It was Tucker's pool. I will never look at it again in the same way. I hear his voice.

"Mama, it's 7:30 in the morning. Let's go. I have my ball. You can drink your coffee outside."

"Yes, Tucker, you are right." And that is what I would do, because I was not going to deny him anything. This little brown dog, with a big smile and an even bigger heart to share, wanted to swim. And swim he did. Did it really matter if his ears smelled yeasty? An ear infection—who cares? That sure as hell wasn't going to kill him. It is not fair that he is not here. How strange it is to wake up and not have our regular routine. I would get up and go into the bathroom. He would wait, but no matter what time it was—and it was usually still dark outside—when I started to leave the room, he would jump down and follow me downstairs, no matter what; until he stopped doing that routinely.

When did that first happen? Did I notice it? What did I attribute that to? Was it a symptom that I missed? Was his body beginning to react to the disease that was going to steal him away from me? We went outside. I often had to go with him because if

I came back inside, he would come back inside with me. If I went out, he went out. My shadow. And he remained with me until he heard my keys jingle. When he heard the jingle, he went back upstairs because that meant I was leaving the house. I would give anything, anything to jingle those keys and see him again. It is Tuesday morning. It has been more than seventy-two hours since I last laid eyes on my beautiful Tucker. I can taste the grief. It is sour. It is bitter. It is evil.

We had a thing. He was my Waze boy. Waze, the GPS app. Whenever he heard that voice, no matter where he was, no matter what he was doing, he would run and jump up on my lap while I sat in my—I mean our—favorite chair. He would settle on my lap into Tucker-time. When I wanted him to come to me, I would sometimes just call to him, "Waze, oh Waze. All set, let's go." And he would come. Waze. My Waze. I might have to use Google Maps now. I do not think I can listen to the Waze voice ever again. I want him back.

Every day I am going to wake up and it is going to be the same. Every day I am going to wake up and there is going to be no Tucker here. No Tucker on the floor, no Tucker on the couch, no Tucker on the bed. No Tucker with his ball in his mouth or his baby or his bone. How does one comprehend that? I can't.

Do I feel relief? I do, but it is such a sad relief.

I had been filled with the worry of his potential pain. That fear of his pain, of his demise, made me come face to face with my own mortality. With the potential mortality of others that I love. Tucker's death has left me feeling so empty, and it is pervasive. I tried hard to live in the moment when we were together. And I faked it. I threw the ball, I tickled him, I called him by all my favorite nicknames, I showered him with treats.

But inside, the future was winning. I know if you live in the present, there can be no fear of the future, but I wouldn't be lying if I told you that in the battle between living in the moment and fearing the future, the future fear won. The anticipatory grief never did lessen; it poisoned my daily life with him. I was worried. And yes, I do not have that worry now. I am not worrying about whether or not the CHOP (chemotherapy) will work, whether or not he'll get pulmonary fibrosis from the Tanovea, or whether skin lesions will occur. No, I do not have to worry about that, but it was never going to be a worry because your cancer snubbed its nose at all those treatments. Your cancer was the vehicle that arrived to take you. And the toll you paid to cross that bridge is my burden, my pain, and my love for you that intensifies with every minute that goes by.

It is a week today, Tucker. A week today since you ate your last meal, took your last swim, sat in the sun with the ball. It is a week ago today that I last looked into your eyes and gave you treats. It is a week ago today that I worried about your panting; was it normal, was it going to go away? You died suddenly, Tuck. I did not expect it. When we took you to the vet, I thought we were going to stabilize your breathing. I thought we were treating you. We did not know. I did not know I had to make that decision. Tucker, I miss you whining for a treat. I miss you jumping off the bed, I miss you pulling me on the leash, I miss you sitting on the steps overseeing your territory looking for movement, I miss you running into the back forty. Bean, I miss you on my lap, I miss your schnozzle kisses, I miss your excitement and the look in your eyes when you saw the new toy in the package or smelled the new container of racquetballs being opened.

I have not yet gone on a ball walk, Tucker. I have not yet walked your territory, your land, to find your beloved balls. I cannot. I leave them tucked away in the woods, under the trees, by the pool. I leave them for you to visit when your spirit comes.

My Tucker, I see you everywhere, yet I see you nowhere. There are sacred places. The cushion tops of the couch. The bathroom floor, which I think became your comfort place as you sickened. It was a cool place for your overheated prednisone body. In the dark, when I would wake, I would see your sleeping outline and walk so carefully into the bathroom, afraid to disturb whatever peaceful sleep you were able to have. I listened. I was always listening. Was your breathing even? Ragged? Too shallow? Too deep? How was your energy level? What did you eat? Did you turn away from it? Would you only eat it from my hand? And Tucky, what were you thinking? Did you know? Did you eat to make me happy? What did you know?

Tucker, there is a fly in the room as I write this. I picked up the swatter, and you weren't here to react the way you always did when you saw a fly swatter. Your nub would go down between your legs and your ears would drop and you would walk away. Afraid of it? Fearful for the fly? I put it down, Tucker. I just let the fly be. I couldn't save you, but I could save that damn fly. It's a week today, Nubby-Bean. One week. Rest peacefully, my best boy.

Love, Mama

WEEK 2

You want to know how I feel? It's been two weeks since I last buried my face into your fur to cement your smell permanently in my mind. Two weeks since I looked into your trusting eyes. Two weeks since I sprawled myself on the floor of the vet to be on your level to kiss your nose. Two weeks since I saw the last wag of your nub. Two weeks and I am still numb. I get up in the morning and am secure in the knowledge that the sun will rise and the sun will set. That is a given, and that is permanent. Our sun is not about to expire anytime soon. I can accept that permanence, but what I can't accept is the permanence of your absence. As I said before, I see you everywhere, yet I see you nowhere. I am amazed at the number of things that have become triggers.

I have a glass at home. It is a nice glass, a scotch glass. It was the perfect size to hold one large round ice cube ball and scotch, but it got repurposed into Tucker's medicine glass. It fit his many daily pills. The glass was clear and made it easy to see what the pills were and shallow enough to reach in and get the pill. I can't look at that glass, I can't use that glass. It has disappeared from the shelf.

We have a pool, and frankly, I avoid looking at it. I am

anxiously waiting for it to close. I look at it and it says Tucker to me. How empty it seems. It does not offer me any relief or respite from the heat. It is a painful reminder. I avoid the dog food aisle. I find that my daily existence starts with Tucker and ends with Tucker. I miss my baby so much. Yesterday, I simply said, "I want my Boykin back," and it triggered the song "Black is Black" *(I want my baby back)* by Los Bravos. Listen to it. That is how I feel. I just want my baby back, and I do not know why I can't have that happen. You know, I belong to many support groups for losing pets and groups that are totally in love (like I am) with Boykin Spaniels. I find solace there, and I find the need to help others get through this.

There is a whirlwind of emotions when you have a dog with lymphoma. You die twice. The first time is when you get the diagnosis because it is terminal. The second is when the disease wins. And the disease always wins. The best we can do, the best we all do, is try the best we can to beat the disease, keep our babies comfortable, and make the kindest decision to let our babies go before the disease ravages them. I am happy and celebrate any positive news about remission, but at the same time, I am jealous. I cry with each of you who say, "it is time" or "we said goodbye." Everyone's goodbye is my goodbye.

The pain is real, but the pain is different for everyone. I truly understand how we are all seeking a miracle. We ask questions, we supplement, we research. We wonder: was it something I did, was it his environment, was there a symptom I missed? If I had noticed it sooner, would the end result have been different? I can't count the number of questions that ran and still run through my mind. I look at dogs on the street, and the first thing that I want to do is run my hands under their necks to make sure there are no external nodes. That is not something I ever thought of before this. I watch happy dogs and wonder how much Tucker was hiding from me. I did not know they instinctively hide their illnesses to protect their pack. I was his pack. David was his pack. He did not need to protect us; we needed to protect him. I miss him so much. The little things. His jumping on my lap, his sitting on the floor with me, his smell, his touch. Why isn't he here?

I am glad that I do not have to fear every movement anymore, wondering if his hind legs will fail. I am glad that I do not have to observe every bowel to make sure it is not bloody. I am glad that I do not have to wonder if he is suffering, but oh, I would give anything for one more snuggle or one more walk. Hug your babies.

Two weeks is an eternity to be without them. I wonder if the pain will ever go away. I wonder when I will be able to look at his pictures and smile instead of cry. His ashes are ready. I have yet to pick them up. The spirit is still alive, but the reminder that my active, happy Boykin is now in a box is raw and caustic. I loved and still love my Tucker, my Nubby-Bean. Like I said, I loved you for your whole life and I will miss you for the rest of mine. Two weeks, Nubby-Bean. I hope you are chasing balls and saying hello to the Chelse, and Molly, and Dexter, and Nala, and Buford. Love you, Baby.

Love,

Mama

WEEK 3

For those of you who know me, you know I write to work through my grief, and if my words provide any help or comfort to others, which I certainly hope it does, then good. There is grace. Three weeks, twenty-one days from the time my best boy Tucky took his last breath on this earth in my lap. Three weeks—such a short time, such an eternity. Time is relative. It depends on your perception.

When I was writing my dissertation, three weeks were never long enough. Three weeks to finish a chapter or three weeks to start another one. Like a pebble in your shoe, those perpetual three weeks until the next deadline were always there.

When I was dieting, it was three weeks until the event, so three weeks at two pounds a week meant six pounds.

As a teacher, August was the perpetual three weeks. Three weeks left of summer until the new school year. But now, time is different. Now, my time is measured in terms of Tucker-time. No, not the Tucker-time I have referred to before, the times when he jumped onto my lap in the recliner chair to rest while I stroked his ears and back. Not that Tucker-time, but this new Tucker-time. Before Tucker got sick or before Tucker passed. That is how I measure time now.

These are difficult times. I am fortunate to have the Boykin Spaniel Nation and the Canine Lymphoma Nation and the Grieving Dogs Nation of people who are so supportive and understanding. God knows I do not think I could get through my days without all of you. And the days are long. They are still so painful. I am still going through the motions. I get up, I get dressed, I go grocery shopping, but always, always there is the fact that Tucker is not here. He is just not here.

I was away last week overnight to help one of my children with my grandson. When I came home and climbed the steps that led to the kitchen, a cruel punch hit me because I knew that when the door opened, Tucker would not be standing there to greet me with his squealing, and his nub wagging, and his jumping up on me, even though he is not supposed to—was not supposed to. But he couldn't help it because I was home. I would sink down to the floor and he and I would just say hello. David was so patient waiting for us to finish because he knew there was just something about my Nubby and me. I have to take a break here because my tears are clogging my eyes. Usually, when we finished our little meet-and-greet, he would run into the living room, and the next minute, he would be on the couch with his ball in his mouth. "Mama, let's go. I do not know how long you have been gone, but it was too long. It's ball time, Mama." And off we would go into the yard.

What do I do without that? Huh? Three weeks. I can't put a time frame on my recovery. I am smart enough to know you can't rush grief or recovery. I know grief is commensurate with love. How I miss his presence. With Tucker, I would happily get up in the morning and go to work and know that when I came home, he would be there. I knew that at night, if we stayed downstairs later than what he was accustomed to, he would try to get us to go upstairs. He would nudge us. Sometimes he would just lie down and sometimes he would just go up and get into the bed himself. He would look at me reproachfully. "You mean you're not coming now?" Oh my, how I wish I had.

People look for miracles. I am not a true believer in miracles, but I sure found myself hoping for one and working toward one when I was treating his disease with chemo. For all you fur parents dealing with lymphoma, keep believing. Maybe it can happen for you. I can't stop hoping that maybe, for someone, their dog's mutated large B-cell lymphoma will be the one to respond to all drugs and give very long remissions or maybe even a cure. We did not experience that.

Three weeks is a long time to think about all the things you are not going to do again with your "favorite hello and your hardest goodbye." I hope, at some point, I will be able to look at his pictures and his videos and smile. I am not there yet. My heart is still so raw and broken and shattered that it is an effort sometimes to go through the day zombie-like, always thinking, why? Where are you?

I loved you and I still love you. Did you know that? We didn't have enough time, Tucker. I bought a life vest for you. I bought the vest, Tucker, because I wanted to introduce you to the ocean this summer and I worried about rip currents. But we didn't do it. Maybe you are doing it over the bridge. I hope you are.

Tucker's remains are ready. I have not been able to bring myself to retrieve them. I will. I have not forgotten. I will not forget you, Tucker, ever. You will always be my best boy, my Lemon-Head, my Tucker-Ridge, my Nubby-Bean.

Swim high, Bean, and Happy Boykin Spaniel Day.

WEEK 3.5

He's home. We have brought Tucker home. There is a sense of relief that he is back with us and home from the hospital for the last time. I have nothing but praise for the staff at the Cornell Veterinary Hospital, but I am glad to be past that grief and horror. As I work through the loss of my Nubby-Bean, I realize that the anticipatory fear of what would happen to him was worse (at least for me) than coming to terms with his absence. I have not yet been able to "unpack" Tucker from the carefully constructed bag that holds his remains and whatever else is in there.

I want to send my gratitude to the Boykin Nation. To Kimberly DeLamar Orsini, who is going to create a beautiful final resting place for Tucker. I shed a tear when I unpacked Loren Vevon's puppy, who looked like Tucker. Courtney Cannon Hardee, who sent me Tucker on a flag that I kiss every day, and Colleen Kearns Hendricks, whose friendship and talent are dear to me. Boykins are special, but Boykin people are the most beautiful people I have ever met. Thank you all for your caring and support as I go through this process. I appreciate your understanding that it takes as much time as is needed.

WEEK 4

I wrote this for you, Tucker. Are you happy and pain-free? Did you catch that squirrel yet? Are you swimming? You are missed more than you can even know.

It's OK. Go Ahead, Cry.

When you close your eyes,
Do you see him in those little black and white shapes that swim behind your eyelids?
Go ahead, keep looking up at the sky, but not when driving—although that is hard.
What are you looking for?
That one cloud that reminds you of his floppy ears?
What about that one that looks like he is lying down with his head up?
No, not that one, the other one.
The one that looks like him sitting up, handing you his paw.
It's OK.
Go ahead, cry. Cry a lot. Cry a deluge.
Don't worry. I promise you won't run out.
Sit in your favorite chair.
Put something on your lap. A book, two books, a

cement block.
Anything that will take away that empty feeling that is now there.
His weight on your lap, his shifting around.
Better to deal with a little numbness
then shift your position.
That would upset the force.
That would make him jump off.
Let that baby stay on your lap.
It's OK.
Go ahead, cry. Cry a lot. Cry a deluge.
Don't worry, I promise you won't run out.
Sit down with that first early morning coffee.
Stretch your legs.
They make it to the wall.
They are not blocked by that sweet sleeping body leaning against your feet.
Then you pull your feet and legs back
To where they were.
You do not take advantage of that extra stretch room.
You leave the coffee and go outside.
You take in the green grass, the warm breeze,
 the few falling leaves that are arriving early
To avoid the rush-hour fall
You breathe
And it catches in your throat
Because you see him
Running through the grass chasing that bunny, or that bird, or that ball.
You see him stop at the side of the pool before it is closed

Searching for the frog he once saw there last month
so it must be there still.
You see him push the ball in the water himself
because you did not heed his command fast
enough.
He brings it to you and shakes himself off
Dropping the ball at your feet.
Your turn.
It's OK.
Go ahead, cry. Cry a lot. Cry a deluge.
Don't worry. I promise you won't run out.
And as those visions flash-dance across your mind,
The questions begin.
Why?
When will the pain go away?
When will you feel better?
Why didn't you have more time?
Why him?
Why does it feel like the world will never be the
same?
Why does it hurt so much?
And how will you navigate this new world?
They, whoever they are, say Time. You need time.
You pray they are right.
It's OK.
Go ahead, cry. Cry a lot. Cry a deluge.
Don't worry, I promise you won't run out.
The world has spun around for 30 days.
30 days missing you.
30 days wishing you were still here with me.
30 days on earth without you.
Rest and run in peace, Tuck.

I am going to be honest. Writing about Tucker is personal and heart-wrenching. When I craft the words, they pour from my heart in cascading torrents. I don't really plan it, and I don't really know what is going to come out until it actually does. That being said, I realize the intensity of the feelings I have, the pain and anguish that I feel, the acute sadness that enveloped me when I lost my dog triggered something deeper. Something that has probably been simmering, dormant like an inactive yet live volcano, and erupted with vigor when I lost Tucker.

I am no stranger to grief. I wrote that I had lost my birth mother, Julia, and my stepmother, Trudy. Both women were loving and caring, and both helped me become the person I am today. But what I did not share are some of the personal truths that surround my experiences of losing two mothers. I lost one when I was fifteen and the other when I was a mother myself in my forties. Loss as a teenager and loss as an adult; two very different time frames, two totally different experiences, two different impacts, but loss is loss.

Daughters who lose their mothers find themselves in very special grief circles. I am not a clinical psychologist, but I can assure you that a teenage girl who is suddenly motherless suffers traumatic grief. I was a teenage girl, and that is exactly what happened. Loss and grief juxtaposed against teenage growth makes it difficult to figure out what world to live in. Grieving your situation while at the same time trying to fit into the teenage need to blend in and not stand out is really hard. Being a motherless daughter at fifteen is definitely not a way to blend in.

Couple that with complicated feelings about your relationship with your mother, feelings of guilt about her death, and you are left with levels of grief that are unfathomable, but they get buried for self-survival. They only become active decades later.

Life moves on, and sometimes you end up being blessed. After my birth mother's death in 1969, my father did remarry. I truly adored my new stepmother. She was loving, kind, and I connected to her in ways I was never able to with my mother. She never tried to compete for my dad's affection, and she did not try to erase my memory of my mother. In fact, she tried very hard to get me to talk and recognize both the happiness and pain I felt as it related to my relationship with my mother. She gave me the freedom to express the feelings I had about my mother. She recognized, appreciated, and understood me. That was key. She understood me in ways that my mother did not. So when she died, I lost more than I think I realized.

I was already a mother myself, and I felt like I had lost both a mother and a friend. My children had lost their Granny. In between raising children and working full-time, I suppose I tried to deal with the inevitable, unanswerable questions. How come I lost another mother? Why? What did I do this time? Why did I have to go through the specific loss dynamics that exist when daughters lose their mothers again? If I were keeping count (which I was), I would have to note two tally marks under Death of Mother Figures: II. And one mark under Death of my beloved fur baby: I. And the pain was not eased because Tucker had four legs instead of two.

WEEK 5

Let's talk a little about time again. Some say time is a human-made construct. It is. Clearly, the planets and stars and nebulae exist and will exist, and they have no concept of time. They just are. Humans invented the construct. The planet rotating on its axis allowed humans to create the construct of night and day. Time is an invention, but it also does not hold a fixed state. Like a non-Newtonian fluid, it changes. If you beat the egg whites for too long a time while making French macarons, the proteins separate, the cookies lose their sheen, and they get dry and crumbly, not moist and chewy. Time matters for macarons. You must follow the prescribed time suggestions to the letter.

And sticking with the French theme, if you underbake a soufflé, you get a soup-like mess; overbake it and it collapses. Time matters for soufflés.

It matters when you need to go to the store. If you get there too early, you can't get in and you have to wait. Get there too late, you have to leave. Time matters for shopping. Want to know when time doesn't matter? It doesn't matter when you are grieving.

It has no meaning. One day, one week, four months,

maybe never. Grief is the most personal event I can think of. In many ways, even more personal than birth. Time counts with birth. You know a new life is going to be brought into the world in nine months, give or take a few days or weeks and some pretty uncomfortable moments. But the problem with grief is you don't know how long it is going to last. I think grief makes people uncomfortable, especially as "time passes." Sympathy and understanding are good and appropriate, but at a certain point, maybe when people think that enough time has elapsed between the death and the mourner's emotional state, people get uncomfortable. They don't know what to say, so they don't say anything. That is okay, but I think their silence is more for their comfort, not the mourner's.

Or the elephant in the room enters and the conversation that flows is often meaningless, random—its main purpose is to ensure that the discomfort around the grief is not approached. Why do I bring all this up? Well, for those of you who have been reading my posts, you might notice a pattern. I always post on Friday.

I always acknowledge the fact that Tucker is dead; however, this is the first time I have actually come right out and said it that way. Not he's gone. Not he's crossed the bridge. Not he's gotten his wings, but he's dead. There it is out there. And I will add something else out there, as stark and naked as my statement that he is dead. It's been five weeks, thirty-five days, 840 hours, 50,400 minutes, and it means nothing. So, in the interest of maintaining the stark portion of this and in the interest of transparency, I will plainly state a fact. It has been five weeks, and

I am not feeling better. I am, sometimes, feeling worse. I miss the life I had when we were three. I did not lose a pet; I lost a goddamn family member. So, there it is. There is no one else on this earth, except maybe David, who wants to see me feel better than me. But. I. Don't. Feel. Better. I don't. And that's the honest truth. I do not think there is a time frame for my grieving. It hurts way too much.

Did You Know

> He cooled himself under the big marsh grass.
> His body on the cool earth, his head sticking out
>   from the towering fronds.
> I called him Tucker-of-the-Jungle.
> All that remains are a few trampled fronds
> Crushed by the weight of the neighboring hydrangea
>   branches
> No longer able to support themselves.
> Did You Know
> He was a sentry
> Sitting at his post, surveying ever so carefully
> The grass, the bushes, the frog pond
> For movement.
> And when he caught a glimpse
> He flew down the steps and into his world.
> All that remains are the empty steps
> Whose purpose seems gone.
> Did You Know
> He had a peculiar fear of big black garbage bags.
> Seeing the box of Hefty bags sent him running
> Somewhere else

That wagging nub now tucked between his legs.
I did think it was funny.
Oh, what I wouldn't do now to protect him from
    that big, old, mean bag.
All that remains is the wish that he could run to me
And fear the bag no more.
Did You Know
There was a bowl of water tucked away for Tucker
In the bathroom of our room
Under the sink
Because I did not want him to travel
Downstairs
At night
In the dark
To find his water bowl.
It was just a plastic breakfast bowl.
All that is left
Are the tears that fall when I see it.
I still have it.
I will not use it.
Did You Know
He liked the snow.
This native dog of South Carolina
This beautiful Boykin Spaniel
Would run in the snow
And lick the snow off the deck
And come in with his fur caked with ice and snow.
Out came the hair dryer
Or a kitchen whisk to capture the snow knots
And he would wait patiently
And then run right back outside.
All that is left are those memories of my snow-dog.

All that is left at all
Are the memories.
Rest in peace, Tucker-Ridge
Because I am still not able to do so.

Poetry is a cathartic genre. It allows you to freely express your feelings without being bound by the conventions of English grammar or punctuation. It is a genre that unleashes parts of your brain that other genres do not. When you write a research paper, you automatically think concretely. Concise and simple words. Stark and functional. Words like epistemology, methodology, and phenomenology. But when you jump into the poetic, your brain goes to a different place, a softer place, an emotional place. I write for my Tucker, and my emotional side moves to the poetic. It comes honestly.

I wrote for my Trudy, my beloved stepmother, whom I often refer to as my mother because of my deep connection to her and for what she gave me. When she died, my emotional side erupted with feelings, and so I wrote, as I usually do.

My Eulogy for Trudy–My Mom

When I was 15, I lost my mother to cancer
I am 43, I have lost my mother to cancer
Two mothers, too many, far too soon.
When I was 15, my world shattered,
Loud and Shrill–like thousands of steel-sharp shards of glass
No longer shining, no longer brilliant
But cruel in their acuteness
Cruel in their deadly sharp edges

Cruel in their ability to pierce the heart

When my world shattered, my heart broke
A wrenching break
Lightning quick
Earth-shattering
Breath-stopping
Reeling in pain, the screaming inside my head
So loud it had to be leaking through my pores
Yet
Who could hear?

I was alone, stranded and desolate
Barely balancing on precipices of craters
Here on Earth
Fathomless craters unseen by those around me
Even those closest to me
Craters unseen even by myself

I surfed along this precipice, seemingly untouched
Taking an occasional stumble in
But managing to pull myself out
Unscathed, but not really
For underneath lived a bubbling, turbulent world of confusion
    and despair.
Who could quench and still the churning waters?

A rose appeared.
A beautiful rose
Unafraid of the turbulence before her
New and fresh and vibrant

Ready to give, ready to love.
Who could see the craters and the person teetering on the edge?

The rose that could see the craters that no one else could
Not even myself.
"Julia," she said, "I have brought you your daughter."
As she brought me to visit her grave.
Who but a rose, unafraid of troubled waters, could
Guide me through the puzzling maze of adolescence
And light the way for the roads ahead
Allowing me to sink a little
But never allowing me to drown?

Who else could say, "Sol, can't you see? Your daughter needs you."
Only a rose could see the turbulent, muddy waters
And bring them to clarity
And change them to a peaceful ebb and flow of a gentle wave.

I am 43 and my world has shattered again
Loud and shrill like thousands of steel-sharp shards of glass
No longer shining, no longer brilliant.
But cruel in their acuteness, cruel in their deadly sharp edges
Cruel in their ability to pierce the heart

You came into my world and healed a gaping wound
Filled my life and the lives of those around me
With laughter again and renewed smiles long forgotten
You opened my eyes to sights I'd never seen before
And filled my heart with emotions I never knew existed

You taught me to talk
You taught me to feel
You taught me to trust with love that was honest
And pure and strong
And unconditional
And yet, your own fears of being lost and alone
And unloved kept you wondering,
"Do I belong? Will I make a difference?"

And so it is for all of us
That turbulence and uncertainty come and goes
Sometimes in voluminous waves
Sometimes in a ripple soft and gentle
Sometimes as a mighty storm
But always there is the rose that stands strong and tall
And sweet
A fragrant and beautiful gift to all who are lucky enough to
    have been touched by her wonder.
So you see
Your fears were unfounded
You indeed made a difference
An enormous difference in my life
In all of our lives
Thank you, Mom.
And Mom, I am wearing red shoes.

WEEK 6

I took my five- and seven-year-old granddaughters off the bus. Kindergarten and second grade. Their parents had recently told them about Tucker. When the seven-year-old got off the bus, the first thing she said was, "Mommy told me that Tucker died. Are you and David sad?"

"Yes, we are. Very sad. I miss him very much. What are you going to miss most about Tucker?"

"Grammy, I am going to miss how he used to stick his schnozzle into the bath when we were in and how he drank the bath water and got bubbles on his nose."

"Me too, honey, me too."

Not long after, while sitting in the kitchen, I asked the five-year-old about Tucker. I told her I was sad that I would never see him again. She said, "Yes, you will. You will see him again."

"Really, do you mean in heaven?"

"No, not heaven. He is in a special place."

"Where is that special place?" She stopped chewing her snack and thought for a moment.

And then she said, "California."

"So does that mean when we play the game vacation and we always travel to California, we will see Tucker there?"

"Yes, Grammy, we will. Do you want to see my doll?"

Out of the mouths of babes. The concept of death. If you celebrate the Jewish New Year, you wish for a new year filled with sweetness and happiness. It is also the time of year for atonement. You self-reflect on how you have wronged others and how you can make amends, ask for forgiveness, and grant forgiveness to others. It is both a time to work towards a good, sweet year to come and make a pledge to become a better person than you were before. I do not believe that is a religious goal. I think it is a human goal. Improve the world. Help others. Do what you can to be kind and giving. Put someone or something before yourself. Give. Do you know this story?

The Star Thrower
by Loren C. Eiseley, *The Star Thrower*, 1978

One day, a man was walking along the beach when he noticed a boy picking up and gently throwing things into the ocean.

Approaching the boy, he asked, "Young man, what are you doing?"

"Throwing starfish back into the ocean. The surf is up, and the tide is going out. If I don't throw them back, they'll die," the boy replied.

The man laughed to himself and said, "Do you realize there are miles of beach and hundreds of starfish? You can't make any difference."

After listening politely, the boy bent down to pick up another starfish and threw it into the surf. Then, he smiled at the man and said, "I made a difference to that one."

How do you make a difference? You reach into your heart and let all the loving kindness that exists within flow out to help others. Do not be afraid that you can't make a difference. Like the young boy in Loren Eiseley's poem, he did what he could. It is the little things, the little acts of kindness, that make a difference. My mothers all gave me something, little pieces from their hearts. Tucker gave me his whole heart.

Tucker, I have not seen you physically for six weeks today, but I see you every day in my heart.

The Exchange

I gave you a ball. A simple blue racquetball.

And you? What did you give me?

You gave me a sense of simplicity. You showed me that a simple ball was all you needed. You did not need a bigger one, you did not need a better one, you did not need what some other dog had. You simply needed that one blue racquetball. And I learned that to chase more means you will never be satisfied. Because if you must always chase something more complex, you will never understand the beauty of simplicity. You will forever be on a hunt for *something* that will make you happy and content. You will never come to realize that you must work on creating that sense of contentment and happiness within yourself.

Tucky, I will find the simplicity around me and the peace simplicity offers. And all of that through a simple blue rubber ball and your unspoken mantra that "Ball is life." Thank you, Nubby-

Bean, for teaching me that lesson.

I gave you a place to sit on my lap. On our chair, in our place. You sat and rested your head on the chair and fell asleep. Breathing rhythmically as I stroked your head, behind your ears, your neck, your back. Your warm, soft fur tickling my hand. Your peaceful slumber and heart beating—matching the rhythm of mine.

And you? What did you give me? You showed me a love so big and so grand that I thought it would burst out of me. You brought forth a feeling of devotion and reawakened my motherly instinct as I watched your sleeping body and knew I would do anything to keep you happy and safe. Your quiet rest in my lap encompassed all that is good in the world. Your comfort in my lap reminded me there was no real need to do anything else at that moment, or rush to any other place, or worry about something that wasn't done yet. Your rest in my lap was the only thing that mattered. Your peace was the only thing that mattered. Everything else—could wait.

Thank you, my Lemon-Head, for teaching me the lesson that there is nothing stronger and more important than loving deeply. It is the greatest gift one can give, and the greatest gift one can receive. And perhaps it truly is the reason that my grief over your death is so intense. To love deeply is to grieve immensely.

I gave you a bone. A simple marrow bone. "Good morning," said the butcher, "I saved a good marrow bone for Tucker." And when I brought it into the house, in the high voice that you knew meant I had a surprise, I said, "Ooooh, look what I have." And you looked at me with those big eyes, the expressive eyes that said, "What? What do you have for me?" and I gave you the bone.

And you? What did you give me? You showed me that it is not the size of the gift or the price. It is not whether or not it is designer this or designer that. It is the love and care one has for another. You showed me what being grateful is. You showed me what being thankful is. And no, you did not say it, but when you took that bone and ran down the steps to that special place that only you knew, that special place to bury that bone, so that you could protect that bone the way I protect you, showed me that generosity of spirit is the greatest gift one can give and receive. Your big eyes were the epitome of that lesson. Thank you, Tuck-Tuck, for teaching me that.

I gave you a dog treat. A simple dog treat.

And you? What did you give me? You gave me a deeper understanding of what it means to help others, to understand someone else's wants and needs, to be trusted. You gave me the realization that I have the power to help. You would look up at me with those expressive eyes, opened wide, filled with hope and trust. Your eyes said, "Please, Mama, please, a cookie for me. I know that cabinet. I know you are sitting at your desk right next to the cabinet. I know it won't take much. Just reach over a little and open it up." And I did because I had the power to help you and the love to want to. I may not be able to solve the world's problems—of which there are many. I may not be able to end the war in Europe, but I could help you, Nubby-Bean. I could help build that trust you had in me, the trust that I would attend to your needs and wants. A trust that is so vitally important that nothing else matters. And you? What did you give me? You gave me the drive to help. You gave me the drive to better the world and to ease the pain of others. So, in your honor, my Nubby-Bean, I will reach out to help others whose hearts are breaking with loss. In your name, Tucker-Ridge, I will help others who are facing the struggles we had together.

Rest in peace, Tucky. Come visit me in my dreams. I need to give you a hug.

The exchanges. I remember a movie called *Love Story*. I remember that one of the lines was, "Love means never having to say you're sorry." No, I disagree. Love means that you can and should say you are sorry, and your partner will appreciate it if it is warranted. In fact, if an apology is required and it doesn't come, love can erode and be replaced by resentment. People who love give each other many things. The give and take does not have to be even. I gave Tucker many things, and he gave me the world.

I lost two moms. The two women were really polar opposites. Julia, my birth mother, was large, unconventional, and eccentric. Trudy, my stepmother, was thin, beautiful, bright, and loved convention, but she, too, was eccentric in many ways. These two women had a titanic impact on me. As I think about exchanges, perhaps it is time to put forth and lay bare the exchanges.

When I write about my mother, Julia, I will be honest and say there was a lot about my mother that embarrassed me. Her appearance was odd. She wore floppy hats and hand-embroidered overalls, often covered with a mink coat. Her shoes were typically torn tennis shoes or combat boots. I can't ever remember my mother coming to school to pick me up dressed like other typical mothers dressed in the late sixties/early seventies. Today, I recognize the eccentricity and the bohemian flavor as something to admire, but not when I was fourteen. However, one thing that I always appreciated was my mom's creativity.

My mother's high energy levels were frequently displayed in behaviors that were exhilarating and fun but also impulsive and daring. She was a determined woman and went after what she believed was right. She fought for just causes. When we were living in Far Rockaway, New York, we did not live far from the beach, and we often went there. I remember her involvement in making sand sculptures with us. We would dig big holes and shapes in the sand. She would mix up bags of plaster of paris, and we would fill the shapes. When they dried, we would dig them up and wash them in the ocean. It was thrilling to see what we had made. We would bring them home proudly. What a wonderful memory. I knew no other people who would create such wonders at the beach. It was as though typical pail and shovel activities were not even considered. I am so glad about that.

Our Halloween costumes were as creative as the limitless boundaries of her mind. There were never plastic masks or cheap polyester costumes. The costumes were made with love, by hand, and were fantastic. Scarecrows made with real straw, ears of real corn, stuffed crows, pitchforks, and bales of hay. Cowgirls, complete with chaps, holsters, cap guns, boots, and fringed vests. And cowboy hats. Gypsy dresses with scarves and strings of colored glass beads. There was joy in preparing those costumes, there was joy in wearing them, and great joy in the pride I felt when I said, "Thanks, my mom made it."

My mother had a command of the language but not always conversationally, at least with me. I am sure there were many times that we talked, but it is somewhat sad that I cannot really remember any warm, heartfelt conversations. However, she did have a way to communicate with me when she recognized my pain. She crafted stick figure picture books designed to help me cope with my childhood fears and troubles. Stick figures that acknowledged my pain and attempted to make it all better. And it did.

I have enormous gratitude for that, but as a writer attempting to make sense of my life and how my mother and I are intricately connected, I wonder why she chose that format. Was it because of her sheer creative genius? Did she make a clear-cut decision based on sound personal knowledge about me that crafting a picture book would be the best way to deliver a helpful or healing message, or was it the only way to communicate because she could not, or did not know how to communicate with me verbally, face-to-face? I am not sure what it is, but here I am, fifty-four years later, publishing my first books. Picture books and this narrative. So, thank you, Mommy.

When Tucker was diagnosed with cancer, I immediately rushed to purchase any book I could that would explain this terrible affliction. I turn to books when I need information. I do not like the unknown, and when I have facts and information, I feel I have a better ability to handle what is thrown at me. And perhaps, on some level, I was bargaining. Maybe the more I learned and understood about canine lymphoma, the more likely it would be that the disease would go away and Tucker and I could resume our happy life–the one we knew before the diagnosis. As I read about nutrition and what a healthy carb-free diet might be able to do, I started cooking. I researched mushrooms and supplements. I paid attention to the internal temperatures of food. I researched the benefits of raw diets. I followed recipes. If a cancer diet was going to help my boy, then bring on the chef's hat.

Cooking is not alien to me. I love to cook and bake. I collect cookbooks. I subscribe to cooking magazines. When the *Food Network* magazine shows up,

I am excited. There used to be a magazine called *The Pleasures of Cooking*, published by Cuisinart in the 1970s. It was in the early days of cooking magazines. There were no ads, and the contributors were famous chefs. It has been out of print for years, but I still have many of them from the seventies. I remember many of the wonderful things I made from those issues. Pots de crème, apricot cheesecakes, fresh brioche, duck confit. All made, all eaten, and all delicious. My issues are dog-eared, stained with sauces from the cooking process, and just dirty, but the recipes are still as good.

Trudy loved those magazines, she loved to cook, and she was a great one. Trudy taught me about cooking, and I cherish all the cookbooks she gave me with her handwritten notes. I learned a lot from her about cooking, and I channeled her teachings when I immersed myself in cooking for my Tucker.

Trudy had an industrial-type kitchen. Open shelves held pots, pans, and pantry items. Colorful canisters, unlabeled, graced the shelves. I remember tasting the mousse she was preparing for dinner. I remember thinking it wasn't sweet enough. I remember sprinkling some "sugar" (powdered garlic) into the mixture. And while I do not remember everything, or frankly anything, about the dinner itself, I do remember the reaction when people tasted the mousse. I do remember the disappointment and dismay at my passive-aggressive action. Did I destroy her dessert on purpose? And I remember that she did not lash out at me or treat me like a pariah. That was the beauty of Trudy. She knew me better than I knew myself, and she demonstrated that in so many ways.

As my mother, Julia, lay in her grave, oblivious to the days, weeks, years that passed without any visits from me, Trudy was not oblivious. As a rule, I am not someone who routinely visits cemeteries like many others who make annual pilgrimages to pay their respects to lost loved ones. Yet, when I do go, there is a sense of calm that befalls me, allowing me to take a step back and reflect.

My mother may have been resting still, but I was not. My turmoil was not resting, and if I did not notice it bubbling, Trudy did.

We were in the car together. She started to talk. "Sheila, I am not trying to replace your mother. I am not trying to steal your loyalty. I am not in competition. And I want you to know you are angry. And being angry sometimes means you act out, but I understand that. I also want you to know your father loves me and I love him, and no matter what happens, that will not change. I am on your side, Sheila."

"Where are we going?"

"To the cemetery. I am taking you to see your mother."

I am fairly sure we had a further conversation, but I'm not really sure. I do remember stopping at the office to get a plot map. And why would I need that? If I were a better daughter, I would know where to go. Why don't I know where to go? We returned to the car and drove past the aisles marked Calm 40 or Spruce 30 or whatever names the cemetery used to mark the locations of lost loved ones. I know it is supposed to ease a troubled heart and provide a serene passage to the spot where your loved one's journey to their final passage is located. But the names did nothing to ease my heart or my anxiety. Why was I so anxious, anyway?

"I am not trying to replace your mother, Sheila. I want you to know that."

Did I know that? I think I did. I remember feeling a great deal of love and affection for this woman who brought me to a place I could not bring myself. The tempest inside, however, was still there, filled with so many emotions dealing with my feelings about my mom. Why did she leave me? Why did she get sick? Why did I feel it was my fault? Why did she make me feel like it was my fault? Was I a disappointment to my mother? Was I a disappointment to myself? Was I disappointing Trudy?

We reached the site. It was hard to find, not because the map was confusing or because we did not know where to go. It was hard to find because the marker was small compared to the larger, more noticeable stones praising the virtues of the departed. Julia's stone was small and insignificant. I know my father felt bad about that stone. It was a stone chosen out of anger for leaving him alone in this world with three teenage girls. Its simplicity is a thorn to my father. It was a gesture of anger for being left to raise teenage girls by himself. A small, nondescript stone for a woman who was far from being nondescript. He was disappointed in himself for that choice, but that was unknown to me when I stood next to Trudy, looking down at the stone marking my mother Julia's final resting place.

How does one make peace with what swirled in my head as I stared at the stone covering the site that held the remains of the woman who gave me life? How does one document the life that existed, the laughs, the tears, the days at the beach, my favorite rocking horse that I covered in towels when it rained, the pink Schwinn bicycle of my youth? Julia Levine Schwartz, the woman who ached because of my unhappiness but was unable to smooth it away. Those picture books she made were large, rough, and made from manila paper. Those stick figures who, through their words, sought to name and verbalize my problems. The stick figures came in the form of sympathetic characters who tried to relate to my feelings and helped me deal with them. And I still have them.

But she did not just have a creative touch for helping me with my problems. She had a way to recognize successes. When I had accomplished something, the Giant Step Award was created and given to me to acknowledge my triumph. Afraid of thunder. A Giant Step Award created and awarded when I got over that fear. Afraid to try something new. A Giant Step Award created and awarded when I did. How do you reconcile the gratitude you feel when you are staring down at a piece of granite flush with the ground?

    I looked down at the stone and the corners of my eyes began to fill, and my throat was suddenly parched. The sobs began. Trudy stood by and watched. She walked away to give me some time alone with my mom. As she retreated, I said, "Please don't leave." Trudy gave me the ability to recognize that I could love her without feeling guilty. She let me know her goal was not to replace the memory of my mother, but to help me deal with my feelings of abandonment.

WEEK 7

I taught middle school English for twenty-six years. I taught students how to read and write nonfiction texts. Many students are quite familiar with what fiction stories sound like. They have been brought up reading fiction from the earliest bedtime stories to fairy tales to favored and cherished classics. Traditionally, nonfiction is not the typical genre read to young children.

Teaching nonfiction text structure is important. For those of you who are starting to yawn, don't leave just yet. Nonfiction is constructed in purposeful ways and can follow any one or a combination of forms. Chronological structures have information presented in order—like timelines. Compare and contrast structures seek to show the similarities and differences among events. Cause and effect structures are relatively self-explanatory. Something happens and a series of events occurs because of the event. But the one I would like to talk about is the problem-solution structure.

Most of my posts have been about the heartbreak and loneliness that encompass me. Even with a full family life with family members ranging in age from about seven months to ninety-nine years, there is an emptiness without Tucker's presence in my daily world. In my last post, I promised that in Tucker's honor, I would do what I could to help others who are suffering loss and do what I could to help anyone dealing with the struggles that I faced as I watched my beautiful Nubby-Bean struggle with lymphoma and chemotherapy. I talked about Nubby-Bean teaching me the importance of viewing the world from different perspectives. I wrote about how his little brown furry body, his deeply expressive eyes, and his head—his lemon-shaped head—moved me both emotionally and philosophically. All because of that little blue racquetball.

And to fulfill the promise I made to help, to put something before myself, to give, I will share my problem-solution map. I hope it helps me solve some of my own personal struggles with his death—and hopefully, it helps someone else with theirs.

PROBLEM SOLUTION

POSSIBLE SOLUTIONS	POSSIBLE END RESULTS

BEST SOLUTION	REASON FOR CHOICE

When you look at the picture, you will note there is only one problem on this chart, but there are multiple solutions. What does this tell me? It tells me that when you are faced with a problem, you are also faced with the challenge of thinking creatively. You are asked to look at the problem and find a variety of ways to solve it. It leads directly to the adage, "If at first you don't succeed, try and try again." For some problems, it may be very easy to come up with a multitude of solutions. For others, you might be hard-pressed to find even one, leaving you to wonder if the problem is permanent.

Will the problem ever go away? Will I get better? Will I live this way for the rest of my life? I am still very new to the cards I have been handed. I am still angry about the cards I have been dealt. I am still trying to bargain—even though I know it won't do any good. But the mind does what the mind does when it is working through pain and grief. And while I am beginning to accept that Tucker is not coming back, I read many posts from other people who are suffering and who say, "I just want him [or her] back." Me too. But the beginning of acceptance is knowing that won't happen, and instead of wishing for something that is impossible, something that can never happen that you think will make you feel better, I have to now try to focus on things that CAN happen to make me feel better.

As I think about the supermarket-sized collection of hurts, I will just highlight a few. Do any of them sound familiar?

1) I am afraid this hole inside me, the hole that appeared when Tucker left, will never be filled. He was such an integral part of my life that his not being here is like a titanic-sized pothole

that is impossible to avoid, and every time you fall into it, you risk damage. Not a broken wheel axle, or a punctured or blown-out tire, but painful heartbreak over and over.

2) I am afraid that I will never feel completely happy again. Yes, there will be happy and celebratory times, but that is different. It is like that one last slice of pie—the one sitting on the counter, smears of the filling beginning to harden on the bottom of the plate. It is that one last piece of pie that everybody wants but will not take. The last slice that cements the reality that sadness, like the last piece of pie no one takes, just stays in the tin and is now my forever companion.

3) I am afraid that I will never be able to stop reliving those last moments. We took him to the emergency vet just for a checkup. I was supposed to go to my fiftieth high school reunion and was uncomfortable leaving for the weekend without knowing that he was okay. He had been panting—a common side effect of prednisone. But I just wanted to make sure. It was really more for my comfort than his. After all, he had gone swimming and was happily retrieving that infamous racquetball. And when they heard his breathing and looked at his X-rays and then came out to tell us, "Possible respiratory failure," we responded, "What!?"

"Cardiac—"

"Wait, cardiac what?"

"Panting pattern."

"Panting problem?"

The technician stated, "The critical care vet looked at his films from June when he was first diagnosed and the ones that were taken two days ago. His lungs are filled with disease. He is not responding to the oxygen we are giving him. His nodes are affecting his breathing. If you leave him here, we can try to stabilize him, but we are afraid that you will get a phone call at 3 a.m. He could easily go into cardiac arrest or respiratory failure. Or you can proceed with humane euthanasia."

"No, oh no. Now? Now? It was just a checkup."

My world blew up. I got dizzy. My stomach lurched, then dropped. I want to add that they were very nice and the delivery of the information was not as harsh as it may sound here, but the end result was the same. We chose kindness, and we kept the promise we made to Tucker that we would not let him suffer, but I am afraid that I will never lose those last moments.

4) I am afraid the triggers that make me think of him will inundate me, and I will realize that everything will be a trigger. And when those triggers hit, they are like gut punches. My breath catches in my throat, that little adrenaline kick in my stomach arrives—and not gracefully, and the weight behind my eyelids pounds and burns as though the tears are knocking each other over to get out. I am afraid that my whole life will be a trigger to think about the grief.

And that is no way to live. So, in the interest of everyone who is suffering, here is my thinking.

PROBLEM: I cannot get the visions of the last hours/moments out of my mind.

SOLUTION: I will find the strength to go through the images, the hundreds and hundreds of images of Tucker in happier times. Meditating with his bunny, swimming with the ball, lying in the grass as Tucker-of-the Jungle, resting on the couch. I will gather those photos and print them out, look at them, hang them up, and make a collage. I will kiss the pictures and have a conversation with each of those happy photos, and they will hopefully come to replace the painful last-moment images in my mind.

PROBLEM: I can't get comfortable with the passage of time. I go through the motions of the day. On the outside, it looks like I am doing okay, but what you see is not the truth. What you might not see is that sometimes, I still feel like an empty vessel. I go through the day and wait for it to end so I can go to bed. And when the night comes in and haunts me, when the night visions of all that was and all that will not be trespass into my mind's eye, I wait for night to end so I can get up. It is a vicious circle.

SOLUTION: I will find the strength to accept the fact that my days have changed. Perhaps I say it out loud. "Why are you gone? We still had so much to do. I wanted to take you into the ocean. I wanted to take you on the lake." And then, how do I fix it? I will find a way to include him in whatever I am doing. I will talk about him to someone. I will take the walk we used to take. I will bring a tissue, stop at his favorite tree, touch it, hug it, and cry. And then I will walk on.

The nights…well. This is a harder one. Dealing with the dark nights is one of those times where finding a solution is not so easy. Sometimes, the nights are as virulent and unforgiving as his cancer was. Invisible chains hold me in bed and I'm tossing and turning because it is black and dark and silent and every silent noise assaults me. I am in full-alert mode. And it is in that hyperstate that the unwelcome thoughts and questions come. Did I miss a symptom? Should I have done something else? GET UP. Go do something. If you have work in the morning, accept that you just might be tired. Find something to do that might help you strip away the anxiety—maybe enough to let you go back to bed and rest a bit. See this writing? It is taking place at 3 o'clock in the morning.

PROBLEM: I can't stop wondering if I will ever stop being accosted by triggers that stop me dead in my tracks. Things that once brought me joy now feel like steel shards. Will I be in a permanent battle with little things? And then, an even bigger question: Will I be courageous and face them or just avoid them?

SOLUTION: There were so many Tuckerisms. His attachment to his Wubba bunny toy that he would hold in his mouth. If you looked closely at his paws, you would see him making biscuits—a throwback to his puppyhood when nursing. His eyes would close, and he would approach a semi-catatonic state as he meditated with his bunny. I used to jokingly wonder if we took him away from his mama too soon. We didn't. He loved sitting on my lap in our chair every day at 4 o'clock—Tucker-time. I have mentioned it before. And the GPS system, WAZE. Whenever he heard the voice say, "All set—let's go," no matter where he was in the house, no matter what he was doing, he would run to me and jump up on my lap and settle down. I am not sure what it was about the voice, but it was failproof. Sometimes, if I wanted him near me, I would just turn it on. But now, whenever I hear the Waze voice, my stomach drops. Do I push past it, or do I use Google Maps?

When I am in the kitchen cooking or cleaning, the television is on in the background. It is just white noise—mostly ignorable until the Chewy ad comes on. And I freeze. The dog is talking to the owner about the price of toys and treats. Tears well. I change the channel. And then there is coming home from some place, any place. Wherever we went, when we got within ten minutes of the house, all I could do was talk about how I could not wait to get home to see him. Would he squeal in delight? That special squeal that brought me down to the floor to be licked and greeted. Whether it is seeing the exit sign on the parkway or the last errand that will bring me home, his not being there to greet me smacks me in the face.

So, now what? Roy Rogers had a horse named Trigger that was beautiful, and I did not have a negative or visceral revulsion to the word "trigger." Not so much anymore. So, I can continue to be a victim of my triggers, or I can stand up to them. Maybe not all of them, maybe not all at once, but some of them, a few, a couple, maybe one.

Chewy—bring it on. I will buy a few Wubbas and donate them to the shelter. Waze—well, her voice was so special to him that I don't know, I might be Google Mapping it for now. And yes, every time I come in, he is missing. There will be no more squeals or dropping to the floor for greetings. But there is the memory of how joyful that was. I will put a picture of him on the wall so I will see him as soon as I come in. I can put a stuffed Boykin on the floor by the door. HEY, who said adults can't have a lovable stuffie? Remember, multiple solutions are available to solve a problem. If at first you don't succeed, try and try again. Keep trying. There is no one right answer to dealing with pain and grief.

What is the point of all of this? The point is this. One of

my favorite authors is Kate DiCamillo. She has written many, many wonderful books, and she loves dogs. My two favorite books of hers are *Because of Winn-Dixie* and *The Tiger Rising*. In *The Tiger Rising*, she has a wise character named Willie May, who has been hardened by her own trials and tribulations, but they helped shape her into a caring and soft human being despite her outside appearance. She is intuitive and speaks the truth. One of her pieces of advice to the young, troubled female protagonist in the story is, "This is it: Ain't nobody going to come and rescue you. You got to rescue yourself. You understand what I mean?" Sistine, the protagonist, called her a prophetess.

The same goes for grief. People might question how long it is taking you to recover. People might ostracize you or begin to think there is something wrong with you if the trajectory of your grief journey does not meet their expectations. People might tell you just to get over it. Or that it is only a dog, for God's sake.

But your journey is your journey. It is so personal and so different for everyone. All of us share the need to heal, and we all want to remember our babies and smile, not fall apart every time we see a picture or hear his or her name. And while time will assist, I am finding that seeking a way to help yourself heal is cathartic. I am going to try to do this every day. I am going to work hard. I hope I will be successful. I hope it will help you be successful in your own grief journey.

Seven Weeks Bean, seven weeks. I hope you are still running free.

Yours in love and grief.

Mama

WEEK 8

Guilt

What does guilt do for anyone? Does it make you feel happy and cheerful? Does it change your behavior? Does it give you a sense of joy? Most likely, the answer to that question is a big, fat NO. Yet, there are so many of us who feel guilty when our pets die. What did I do wrong is one of the first questions that traverses your thinking. Then there are the many should have, would have, could haves that are waiting in line to assault you. I should have stayed home with him. I could have missed that game. Maybe when he wasn't really eating that much last month, maybe that meant something. Maybe I should have done something. We have all done it.

When Tucker stopped sleeping on the bed with us, prior to his diagnosis, I thought it was simply because it was cooler on the bathroom tile floor. Maybe he needed a haircut. Or maybe he knew on some canine level that he was sick and instinctually moved away from us to protect the pack. Whatever it was, I look back and realize that sleeping on the floor *was* something because it was a radical change of behavior. What could I have done? Should I have taken him to the vet earlier? Would that have made a difference? And should I feel guilty about it? Do we have any control over how much guilt we feel? What exactly is guilt? It is feeling self-conscious. It is feeling a sense of distress about something you think you did to cause a negative outcome. You worry that you have done something wrong, and you are not sure that people will view you the same, or more importantly, you won't view yourself the same.

Guilt can also stem from the belief that you have failed to fulfill expectations—whether they are yours or someone else's. You are a failure. You do not deserve to be loved. You have let someone down. It's true that the reality of the situation is that you may actually have done nothing wrong. Your guilt may not reflect the effort you have put into whatever actions you engaged in. But sometimes the reality of what happened is *not talking* about what you think happened.

Some common causes of guilt include surviving trauma or disaster. This idea seems to fit into how we feel when a beloved pet dies. It is a trauma; it is a disaster. We feel guilty because we thought we had more power to control the situation than we did. I know I felt like that. I tried to play catch-up. Okay, I will make homemade food, I will find the best supplements, I will watch every move he makes like a hawk. I will record it all very neatly in my journal. It was as though every chicken liver I cooked, every shiitake mushroom I boiled, every ounce of turkey tail I used would be enough. If I followed the recipes, if I read the books, if I made the food with love, then surely, surely, like the ancient Hebrews who marked their homes with blood, cancer would pass over my house and leave my Tucker alone.

I figured the more love I poured into his post diagnosis care, the more likely it would be that he would be the one to cheat the Grim Reaper. It didn't work, obviously, but the one thing I can say is that I don't feel guilty.

I became incredibly vigilant. I started walking and recording his bowel movements—by writing down my observations and sketching them. Again, I wanted to make sure that I caught every change. If I needed to change his diet or give him medication or call the vet because of a suspected GI bleed, I would have all the supporting data. I am no stranger to data. I had to collect more data than I ever thought possible when I wrote my dissertation. It was as if boatloads of data, vigilance, and care would save him, but it did not really matter because no matter how detailed my notes were or how careful I was with his food, his cancer metastasized. And I can say again that I don't feel guilty.

Guilt can consume much like a cancer, but if you can release yourself, it will help. Unless you are an animal abuser, which you are not—by the very fact that you are on these grief sites—feeling guilty is something that many of you are feeling. Self-reflect, because under careful scrutiny, you might just find that you really do not have anything to be guilty about. One cannot heal if one is drowning in guilt. You did or are doing the best you can.

Earlier this week, I was taking a walk for the first time in a few days since it has been dumping rain. I made a promise to Tucker that I would walk right into my triggers. That walk we took early in the mornings when there were no cars and even fewer people was one of the most special times. We walked and stopped at the cluster of trees with a stump. He loved the three trees that made up that cluster, and he marked all three. The trees are about a mile from the house, and I noticed that his panting was becoming increasingly labored. As his disease progressed, we would stop at the tree. I would sit on the stump, and he would lie down on the ground—something he never did when he was well. When he was healthy, if I had stopped walking for a moment, he would just stand there tugging on the leash. But when he no longer did that, he took advantage of my stopping to lie down. We rested together.

I sat on the stump and thought of Tucker. I decided that I had to somehow make that tree his. I will not destroy the tree by carving his name on the bark like old-time lovers carving their initials. I was not sure how I would do it, but I knew I would find a way to make that tree his. He will continue to live there. The idea made me smile. I did not feel guilty about taking that walk without him. I did not feel that taking that walk alone would be a testament to my forgetting him. I think many people feel that if they move on with their lives, they will forget their furry friend. That can never happen. No, the walk was made to honor him. And on Wednesday, I walked past the tree and hung the plaque that I made for him. And on Thursday, when I walked past it again, I smiled. Yes, there was a tear there, but I smiled just the same.

As I think about the progress of my grief journey, I am drawn to the metaphor of big amusement parks. There are certain rides in amusement parks that affect you physically and emotionally. There is a very popular ride in water parks. People are standing in a large group inside a relatively shallow pool. They are all underneath a very large bucket. Water pours into the bucket. At some point, the literal last straw occurs, and the bucket tips over, drenching everyone who is standing underneath the bucket. Since there is no visible timer or clock ticking off the minutes that will give you the warning, you are inevitably surprised when the water dumps on you. Screams of delight? Or shock? Whichever reaction is displayed is indicative of how you are feeling.

How does this relate to anyone who is suffering with grief or experiencing the struggles of having a sick dog or any pet? The adrenaline gathering in your body as you uncomfortably wait for the water to spill is how I felt every time the oncologists came out to the waiting room at the hospital and took Tucker in the back. Waiting for them to do his blood work, check his nodes, and whatever else was happening behind that scary door felt exactly the same as anticipating the water drench. I sat, paced, or stood there waiting for the deluge of information that would assault me when they came out and moved us into the consultation room to await the doctor.

"Nodes are bigger, white blood cell counts are too high or too low, still anemic, protocol failing…" That anticipatory fear made my stomach fall, just like the rides that mess around with G-forces.

You know those rides? The large, high roller coasters that drop suddenly with so much force you feel your organs shifting up into your throat? Well, that is actually happening. Your internal organs are floating around inside your body. Some of the organs are connected with ligaments that keep them more firmly in place, but others are a little looser and filled with liquids. Under regular circumstances, your internal organs all press together because of gravity, but when you are on a roller coaster, you are in a free fall. That means there is very little force on your body, so it is like your organs are weightless. It is like everything is falling individually, and that is what causes that sudden sinking feeling. Everyone is surprised by that sinking feeling. The sick feeling that swirls around in your stomach and you just can't decide if you are going to throw up or not. That sinking feeling. It is the same feeling when you get that bad news, the news that lets you know your pet's illness or cancer or condition is terminal. It is that same sinking feeling that you have when you realize there is nothing you can do to change the outcome. Those who are able to afford whatever treatments might be available are the lucky ones, but even if you can't, you still do not have to feel guilty.

Loving your babies the way you do is enough for them. While they are an important part of your life, it is true that you are their whole life and they know it, on a canine level. You know, one thing we are all guilty of is making our dogs/pets human. We anthropomorphize our pets. We talk to them like they are humans. We equate our feelings with theirs. We believe they think like we do, but they do not. They are not angry and saying, "How could you do this to me? How could you betray me like this?"

They are not offering alternative treatments. They are not involved in any of the heart-ripping conversations with the vet or the oncologist or cardiologist or kidney experts. They trust that you will make the right decision—and you do. There is no reason for guilt. It is a common expression, one that is heard a lot on these grief websites: "Better a day too early than a day too late." I believe that is true. I could have left Tucker at the hospital. It was a Friday night, and no oncologists were on call. I could have left him there, hoping for stabilization. I could have left him there and hoped that another Elspar treatment would work to reduce his nodes from pressing onto his lungs, making it hard for him to breathe. But why? He was not responding to any treatment. He was agitated in the ER. The oxygen was not helping. The sedative was not helping. I made a decision. I do not feel guilty. In fact, I do not feel guilty about any decision I made. I believe the absence of guilt is on my side in this healing journey.

Tucker, it is eight weeks and two months to the day that you left. I still cry daily. I still think of you all the time. I still miss you. It is still silent when I walk into the house, but yesterday, when I was talking about you to Frank (remember Frank? He called you Tucky Boy), I smiled. I showed him some pictures, and I smiled. You brought so much to my life, Nubby-Bean. How can I not smile when I think of you? And I will continue to love you and miss you for the rest of my life.

Love you more, Mama

I started this post thinking about guilt. Guilt is a very toxic emotion because it doesn't promote healing. What good does guilt do? Guilt doesn't make you feel better. There is a difference between how I feel about Tucker and how I felt about my birth mother, Julia. I feel no guilt about anything I did with

Tucker. I don't know if I can say the same about my feelings about Julia. Thinking about my birth mother is a mixed bag for me. She loved me, but she did not understand who I was. On some level, I always knew that, and I think it shaped me. And what is interesting is that my dad, who at this writing is ninety-nine and still alive, tells me it was true. An honest man who I am very close to confirmed that my mother had a better connection to my sisters than she had with me. She loved me, but maybe not as much as I needed.

Maybe it wasn't unconditional–but Tucker's love was. Is there something there? Something that needed to be or was fulfilled with the unconditional love from the dog that gave me what I may not have received from my birth mom? I can't ask him and I can't ask her. I can only ask and search my heart for the answer to that.

Where does the dividing line between grief and trauma begin? Which came first? Are they related? Did the trauma of losing a parent at fifteen fuel the grief? Or did the grief over my Tucker trigger the trauma that was already there? At this writing, it is fifty-four years since my birth mother passed on December 29, 1969. Fifty-four years is a long time. Decades upon decades have passed without me paying any attention to how my birth mother's and stepmother's deaths ultimately affected me. Maybe it is time.

As I think about the stages of grief, I can see some parallels with how I felt about all three losses. Some of the memories I have are sharp and unpleasant, others more blurred with the passage of time.

I was shocked when my birth mother died. It was 1969, and my younger sister and I were away in California visiting our aunt when we were called home because our mom had taken a turn for the worse. She had been in the hospital for six weeks and we were sent away for our Christmas break, or so I thought. I want to add that in a conversation I recently had with my dad, I learned something new. At the time my mother was ill, my father was building a business and commuting back and forth from New York to Puerto Rico. My mother's sister, my Aunt Bessie, lived in Los Angeles. My sister and I both thought we were going off to visit her because it would be a good vacation. What I recently learned was that we were being sent to California for an undetermined amount of time because my dad felt that with my mom being in the hospital and his working and traveling, he could not care for us. I asked him, "Dad, if Mommy had not taken a turn for the worse and she was still in the hospital when the vacation ended, would we have stayed in California, school be damned?"

He responded, "Yes." Now, while that new piece of information, fifty-five years after her death, did not change anything, it was something that I had never known. But memories fade. I phoned my sister and asked her if she had known that fact. She, too, said she had not. It didn't change anything for her either, but she was also surprised.

When we landed at the airport, we were told that she had passed away an hour earlier. I had not seen her in six weeks, and I remember falling to the floor at the airport. Somehow, we all made it out of the airport and into a car. We were driving from JFK Airport to New York Hospital in Manhattan. When we arrived, I insisted on seeing her. Standing outside her room, the nurse tried to stop me from going in, but I pushed past her. On the precipice of the doorway, there was a brief moment when I was teetering. It was like playing a game of "Mother May I?"–may I take one step in? I took a step in and was engulfed in my new reality. I was a motherless child. My mother was lying on her back in the bed. I approached her. Her eyes were closed. How could she just be lying there?

Surely, she knew I was there and would open her eyes. Surely, this was just not real. I took a second step closer, entering the room a little more. I was suddenly aware the dull, cool, shaded gray tone was not the room's color but hers.

I stared at her face. How long does it take for the color of life to drain from your face when you die? And what is that color anyway–the one after the color of life disappears? Once that drains away, what is the one that remains? What would you call it? Gravestone Gray? Ghostly White? Rest in Peace Pearl?

I crept slowly toward the bed and peered down at her face. She didn't look all that peaceful to me. She didn't appear to have that my-pain-is-gone-now pallor. There did not seem to be any rest in that face now that she had entered her eternal rest. There was just a stone-cold face, not at peace, not at rest, just there. I was drawn to the wrinkles on her forehead. I moved closer and looked closely at her. I bent down. I touched her skin. It was cold. I shivered.

"Mommy. What happened? We didn't say goodbye. I wanted to tell you about Aunt Bessie and the candy and the little bottles we collected and about the plane. Mommy. What happened? I am sorry, Mommy."

I leaned down and placed my hand on her forehead and stumbled back. Her skin was cold and damp, and I was not prepared for how it felt. The dead coldness lingered on my fingers, and I tried unsuccessfully to wipe that away.

I could not bring myself to kiss her. I knew I should have, but I was too afraid. I left the room and rejoined my dad and my sisters. I suppose this stays with me because it is a traumatic event to see your mom lying dead in front of you and realize that if you had only gotten there an hour earlier, you would have seen her.

If I had only gone to visit her more than once in the six weeks she was hospitalized, I would have had more time to have her as my mom.

If I had only been more worried about her than I was about being popular, she would have loved me more.

If only, if only, if only.

If only I had made it easier for her to love me, maybe she would still be alive. All those times when she started to cry because she couldn't help me, and when she cried, she coughed, and when she coughed, she got sick and turned red in the face. And it was all my fault. If only I was more popular like my sister. If only I didn't need to be liked. If only I could have just been happy. If only I had just kept my mouth shut and not troubled her with my problems. Guilt. What is it good for? Absolutely nothing. Credit goes to The Temptations.

WEEK 9

I post weekly about losing Tucker. Earlier this week, I viewed a post on the Jack McAfghan healing pet loss site. If you are not familiar with it and you are in mourning, you should look into it. There was a post by someone who was recounting his bad dream. The brilliant healer behind the Jack McAfghan healing books and site answered, explaining that as you heal, your dreams will become more pleasant and filled with love.

That made me think. Why hadn't I dreamed of Tucker? In one of my posts, I asked him to come visit me in my dreams because I needed to kiss him. But eight weeks and one day have passed and still no dreams. Why? I began to wonder about the timing of dreams. Perhaps you do not dream right away because it is too painful. You have to live your waking life without the loved one, so why make it a double tragedy by dreaming about who you lost? If you could not have a dreamless night, you would be a prisoner of your pain.

Does the mind do that on purpose? Does that happen to everyone? Does it happen to any of you?

Well, on Saturday, October 7, I had my first dream. It was not enjoyable. It wasn't one of those dreams that had you hoping that you would fall back asleep quickly and get back to that dream. It wasn't one of those dreams that you hope you will have again. In this dream, Tucker was lying down on the ground. I was lying down next to him. Actually, I was lying perpendicular to his body. I remember it being the same exact pose we were in when they administered the drug that would peacefully take him away and leave me shattered. In the dream, I remember feeling his body and burying my head in his brown, soft, curly fur. In the dream, I said to myself, "Yes, this is what he feels like and smells like. He is so soft." He was not dead, but he was. It is hard to explain because that is the problem with dreams. They are not always sensible. In the dream, I was being asked to wake him up. Everyone around me thought he was sleeping, and they were telling me to wake him up, but I knew he wasn't getting up. People said, "Get down and wake him. Whisper in his ear." I got down on the ground and tried to wake him, but I knew it was useless, and the more I tried, the more I knew it was hopeless. The more people pressured me to wake him up, the more I couldn't. Instead, I was the one who woke up, my heart running out of my chest as fast as it could to escape. It was 3:10 a.m. and I was finished, done, kaput. The sleeping train had left the station, and I was not on it. I got up and went downstairs.

My twenty-six-month-old grandson was sleeping. David was sleeping, and I was wide awake. As I sipped my coffee at 3:25, I thought about the dream. Why did it come that night? What was it trying to tell me? I have been writing a lot about doing my best to move on, to turn the hurt and pain into action that might mend my broken heart. I know my heart will never be completely healed. It will always be scarred, but I know it is important to try. That being said, the healing process feels a little like the game of hopscotch. You know that game. You put two feet on the ground for the two spaces that are next to each other and then hop to the next space because you can only put one foot in a single space. At the very end of the hopscotch board (hand-drawn with pastel-colored sidewalk chalk), you have to hop around on one foot to turn around and hop back to the other end. Inevitably, you will stumble and have to start over.

Remember Candyland? The original board had a Plumpy, I think. Or maybe it was Lord Licorice. If you landed on him, you had to go all the way to the beginning again. It was a setback. Two steps forward, one step back. I am having a bit of a setback as I pass the eight-week mark on the way to the nine-week mark that Tucker has been gone.

Over the changing table, there is a photograph of Tucker. My grandson looked at the picture and said, "Tahker." From the mouths of babes, it made me miss him all over again, just like it was day one. When any of my grandchildren came to sleep over, Tucker would sit in the bedroom waiting for me to put the babies to bed, and then he would follow me out of the room. In the morning, the first place Tucker would go to was the closed bedroom door where the babies slept, and he'd wait for me to open the door. He would run in to stick his schnozzle (his snout) into the crib. And for a few days after the babies left, he would still go to the back bedroom looking for them. Tucker was a part of the family and wanted to be near every member of the family.

On Sunday morning, the day after the dream, my grandchild saw a pillow featuring Tucker's face that my daughter had made. He looked at it and said, "Tahker."

"Yes, that is Tucker. Would you like to hold him?"

"Yes. I walk." He wanted to give Tucker a ride on his toy lawn mower. I gave him the pillow, he put sunglasses on Tucker, and he took him for a walk. It made me cry.

In addition to taking care of my grandchild, I was also watching my daughter's dog overnight. It was the first time I had a dog in the house since Tucker died. I needed to take her outside, and I couldn't find her leash. Between the clothes, toys, and other stuff, I couldn't remember where I had put it. The only leash I could find was Tucker's, which was hanging over a charcoal pastel portrait that my dad had given me as a present. I reached for it but hesitated. I did not want to take it down. I did not want to use it. An old, frayed, olive green, knotted leash. It was Tucker's leash. Somehow, the leash felt sacred, but I had no choice, so I used it. Later that day, I dropped the dog off at my other daughter's house. Dottie, the dog I was sitting for, was using Tucker's leash. My daughter lives nearby and I see her often, but I was obsessed with getting that leash back and hanging it where it belongs. It's not as though the leash was going to disappear. It is not as though I was never going to see that leash again. It's not as though I needed it to walk Tucker, but I had to find Dottie's leash and get it back to her so I could get Tucker's leash. I am not sure what the obsession was, but maybe I needed to have solid, concrete, material objects that were his, that are his. That need seems so opposite from the spiritual connection I am trying to have with my Tucker.

That brings me to my intense need to have concrete

manifestations that represent Tucker. I have quite a few, yet I am having difficulty "arranging" his memorial. I still have his remains and his paw print in the bag I picked up weeks ago from the veterinary hospital. I can't unpack it. I am having a beautiful stained-glass portrait made. A wonderful artist and Boykin nation member, Colleen Hendricks, is crafting, with love, a memento for me of my Tucker. And I am having a fantastic, beautiful urn created by another wonderful woman in the Boykin Nation family, Kim Orsini. She is the most talented potter. When she told me his urn was almost finished, I felt happy and scared at the same time. Happy that soon I would have his final resting place and scared that I would have his final resting place. Does that make sense to anyone?

I ordered two stuffies from Cuddle Clones, a company that creates the image of your pet. I sent pictures and gave them information about Tucker. The images of dogs they have created juxtaposed against the images of the real dogs that are advertised on their site are amazing in their likeness. I ordered two. One of Tucker sitting up and one of Tucker lying down. I couldn't wait to get them. And they arrived, but I didn't open them yet. I am too afraid.

I am adding this addendum at thirty weeks. I still have not opened the Cuddle Clones. They sit in the corner of the room. I am still afraid. I am afraid the likeness will be so real that my heart will break again. I am afraid they won't look anything like Tucker, and my hopes will be shattered, and my heart will break again. And the remains are still in the container that Cornell Hospital put them in. His paw prints are still unwrapped. The sympathy card from the hospital is unopened. All these things still rest in the bag on the shelf.

I have his rainbow candle. I have his pictures. I have unopened sympathy cards. I have Boykin shirts I haven't worn. I find myself on Boykin sites looking at glasses with Boykin pictures and Boykin bottles of wine. I am constantly searching Marshalls for dog figurines that look like Boykins that I can paint brown. I have three statues and four bookends. It is as though all these Boykin things are needed to fill the hole that my Boykin, Tucker, left in my heart when he left.

I know, intellectually, that no number of "things" will fill the hole. I know the only thing that will really fill the empty hole is love. Love that was freely given. Love that was complete. Love that was pure and love that was real. That kind of love does not go away. That kind of love does last forever. And while Tucker's physical presence is gone, my love for him is real and here. Sometimes, the love I have for him is so real I feel it. It floods my body, and my heart swells. And when it swells, the hole gets smaller. I am nine weeks into my loss, but the love never leaves. The love only gets bigger and stronger. And the love and the memories will fill that hole of grief with joy.

Tucky, Lemon-Head, Bean, you are missed more than you know by everyone. Nine weeks, my boy. Nine weeks. I hope you are swimming and chasing your blue racquetballs every day.

Love, Mama

WEEK 10

Inventory

When I was a good deal younger, I worked in retail. I was a manager of a housewares department in a major department store chain that no longer exists. The hours were bad, and the pay was worse, but I was living in New York City and life was exciting. One of the job responsibilities was taking inventory. We did that after store hours and it often lasted pretty late into the night, but back then, my nights started way later than they do now.

The inventory process was pretty rote. We counted the large items by hand, but for smaller items, in bulk, we did it by weight. We would gather fifty or one hundred (I don't remember) spoons or forks or whatever other loose stock we had and figure out how much 100 forks weighed. We then weighed the remaining pieces to determine how many pieces we had. Inventory was simply counting what we had enough of, too much of, and what we needed.

Inventory. I have another connection to inventory at this time of year. As soon as Labor Day passes, you wake up, and it is Thanksgiving. Thanksgiving is my favorite holiday. It is the only holiday that I try to claim for my family. It was Trudy's favorite holiday, and when she passed, I took it on. My mom's Thanksgiving was a beautifully orchestrated holiday. The details were always exquisite. Chestnut chocolate purees and ginger carrot soup, individual flowers at each plate, and beautiful place settings. China and crystal glasses that I now own and cherish. Fantastic desserts. A true celebration.

I took on Thanksgiving with my own flair. I am a bit quirky, and it shows. I have chocolate turkeys scattered around. I have a large, five-pound chocolate turkey that is the centerpiece. It sits on a plate with autumn-colored gummies that look like stuffing. Most of my family doesn't eat turkey. We either do not like the flavor or follow a vegan lifestyle. I use multicolored plates with a fall motif, including autumn leaves or pumpkins. Everyone gets a different colored glass. Different tables with different tablecloths, bling on each table. Table bling. Turkey candles, duck candles, goose candles, pumpkin candles. It is a potpourri of fun. Everyone fills out an annual card that asks what they are thankful for. Things do not always match. I want it to be celebratory.

I have a recollection of the last Thanksgiving that Trudy threw. At each of the Thanksgiving dinners, she and my dad made toasts and welcomed all the guests. She was never happier than at Thanksgiving. She was always beautifully dressed, and making sure that her guests were taken care of and welcomed was her only concern.

Trudy never allowed bottles of soda or ketchup on the table. Everything had a special container. Beautiful pitchers housed all liquids. Little, teensy dishes held pats of butter or salt. Little bowls with miniature scoops or spoons to dish out the condiments. But at that last Thanksgiving, there were some noticeable differences that definitely hinted at her illness and her preoccupation with chemo and doctors and wondering how long she had left. There were no fresh flowers on the table. There had always been fresh flowers. Often, each guest had a personalized vase with personal flowers. I believe there was soda on the table. But when there was, it was poured into a glass from the kitchen away from the beautiful table. Two little things that were titanic. It was a signal that something was wrong, that the tradition of her beautiful and graceful meals was coming to an end. When she was well, little details like individual vases and flowers would never have been missed.

Trudy gave me the world. I have to inventory her part in my life as life-changing. I do not know how my life would have been different without having had her in my world to love me, to give me strength and confidence. I loved her sense of elegance and, in many ways, her vanity.

Unlike my birth mother, Julia, who did not care much about her physical appearance, Trudy did care. And it became a family joke that whenever an event was going to occur, her first response was, "What am I going to wear?" She passed before her sixtieth birthday, but she had said, "What am I going to wear?" And when the millennium was coming, and the idea of a huge party was still only in the thinking phase, "What am I going to wear?" was a question.

I appreciated that part of her because I felt the same way. I was always interested in clothes, makeup, and hair, but my mother was not, and that part of my life was not recognized. It was just not a part of her DNA. I was always more girly-girl than my mom. I was enamored with canopy beds and rhinestones. I still am. I liked frilly clothes and vanity mirrors. I liked makeup; Yardley comes to mind. I don't think they exist anymore. I liked princess crowns and fancy crystal chandeliers because they were shiny and glittery. All these things that I liked helped me try to define who I was on the inside because, in the unspoken lessons a mother passes on to her little girl about being a little girl from her most important role model, her mom, was missing in my education.

But Trudy saw it, recognized it, and promoted it. And I am forever grateful. She must be considered a true positive in the inventory of good people.

In a divorced family with adult children and spouses, decisions about where to go for holidays are always something that can easily stir discomfort. Decisions have to be made; who is going to be insulted; who is going to get mad if we don't come? I don't take an inventory of who comes and who doesn't. If you can attend, then I will count you in the inventory of loved ones who will share the moment, and if you can't come, then I will count you in the inventory of loved ones who might attend in the future.

Inventory is an accounting. It is a way to manage. It is a way to assert control. But is it really? Or is it just an illusion? Retail inventory is used to determine what is needed to turn a profit. Educational inventories measure skills or even intellectual capacity. It is an accounting of cognitive abilities. And there are inventories for emotional capacity. An emotional quotient inventory is used to determine an individual's social and emotional intelligence and one's ability to function.

In an attempt to "manage" or "control" my fluctuating emotions, I am going to try to inventory the ebb and flow of my healing process ten weeks in. Ten weeks. It is hard to believe. If you have been reading my posts over the last ten weeks, you know I have referred to time and how it has no meaning when dealing with grief. Nonetheless, just like retail outlets who engage in quarterly inventories, I am going to perform an inventory. And this is the correct week to begin. As an educator, I will stick with the academic calendar that defines a quarter as ten weeks.

Last week was a very tough week. It was the type of week where things would seem to feel okay, but then all of a sudden, a thought would pop into my mind. Thoughts like "geeze, I am never going to see him again." Or "next summer, there will be no pool for him." Well, there will be a pool, but not for him. It would suddenly hit me again that the only way I could ever see Tucker again would be through the many, many photos I have. Yes, there are videos, but I have not been able to look at them yet. It is similar to being unable to unpack his "remains package." The stark realization that his absence is a forever absence comes back with a vengeance.

In an attempt to categorize what I am going to inventory, I have to classify the jungle of thoughts. In housewares, it was easy. There were soft goods and small electric appliances and bakeware and cookware. Easy. How does one try to categorize the many things that Tucker gave me, that I experienced, that I miss?

One inventoriable category would be comfort. On cold, dark, rainy nights, when he curled up on my lap or put his head on my stomach, I felt warm and comfortable and safe. No matter how hard the wind blew, his soft fur and sweet doggie scent were all I needed. I am no stranger to sadness. I have been sad and cried about other things before Tucker got sick and died. I have children whom I cried for when they were sad and struggling. Is it true that you are only as happy as your most miserable and unhappy child? Tucker made me feel better if he sat with me and licked the tears off my face. His presence eased my pain. I have to inventory that. I was lucky to have that.

I want to inventory laughter. Did you know laughter improves your life? It reduces the production of stress hormones and boosts your immune system. Sometimes it is very hard to smile and laugh in the world we live in, but Tucker made me laugh when he would not let go of his ball, even when he barked. His bark was muffled, but he would not drop the ball. That made me laugh. He had this weird communication with his bones. He would lay his two front paws down, his butt in the air, and push the bone with the side of his schnozzle (snout), talking to it. It was hilarious, and it made me laugh. Laughing is good for you, so thank you, Tucker, for boosting my immune system. I have to add that to my inventory of good.

Togetherness. Sometimes it feels that the distance between people is growing at an exponential rate. The more we network, the more we can connect almost instantaneously on the web, the farther and farther apart we become. Have you looked around you when you are out? People sitting next to each other and across from each other, and no one is talking to each other. They are all buried in their phones. They are as close as they can be physically, but they might as well be galaxies apart. The connectedness is gone, the intimacy is gone, the togetherness is nonexistent. But Tucker did just the opposite. He created togetherness. He loved nothing more than being with the family. He would hop up onto everyone's lap when they were on the couch. He would settle in and start schnozzling anyone who was around. His tail was constantly wagging. He would bring his ball to anyone. That was a sure sign of his love for you. If he trusted you enough with his blue racquetball—then you were family. You couldn't help but tussle his fur and throw the ball. And he never wanted to be away from us. If David and I were standing together, he would jump to form a group hug. I would always say it was our little *fambily*. He brought everyone together, and that is a good thing. It is a positive in the inventory.

I still hold in my mind things that I do not want to inventory. I have written before about the shock we felt when we heard his diagnosis, of the shock we felt when we were trying to deal with the fact that his disease was incurable. I still hold his last day in my mind. We did not know it was his last day. I still hold the questions as to whether or not I hugged him enough that day or kissed him or threw the ball enough. I still hold the caustic memories of the shock we felt when the vet suggested that we humanely release him. I still hold his last minutes in my mind, but I do not want to inventory those. I want to inventory the joy he gave. The joy he spread. The love that we shared.

Memories will need to move from the inventory of pain and loss into the inventory of joyful reminiscence. Tucker-Ridge. It has been ten weeks since I last threw your blue racquetball into the water and hugged you. I hug you daily in my mind. Keep running and swimming and being you. Rest in peace, my Nubby-Bean.

When I Think of You

When I think of you
My heart still weeps
My heart still mourns
My heart still questions "the why."
There was nothing I could do
We could do
To change the outcome.

When I think of you
I still feel you lying on my lap, shaking when the thunder booms
I still hear you squealing in delight when I come home and open the door to the hallway
I still reach out to touch your head when I wake and ache when all I touch is air
I still see you sitting at my feet, gazing up soulful, begging for that cookie.

When I think of you
My heart still weeps
My heart still mourns
My heart still questions "the why."

There was nothing I could do
We could do
To change the outcome.
When I think of you
I still cry. I still wish we had more time.
And oh, how I wanted to keep you here.
But that was not to be.

So I relive the moments we had
And then I smile
When I think of you.

WEEK 11

My writing has touched people. Some people say to keep writing because they need to see their feelings validated by someone else. Some people say they have the same feelings but can't express them. Others say that the words are too real, and they need to abandon the writing because it is too painful. Others say I should write a book. I can say that I am simply here to work through my own wondering and grief about losing a member of my family—and he was, just as your fur babies are members of yours. And if my words, bare as they may be, help anyone else, then I consider that an added blessing.

My granddaughters came to spend the weekend. It was the first time since we had received Tucker's diagnosis. Why did so much time go by without a visit? Well, one reason was that we were consumed with taking care of Tucker, and the other reason was that we had a rescue dog at the time, Rocky, who was not comfortable around little children, a working dog who viewed small children as sheep to herd. We had to minimize the small children who came to the house until Rocky was rehomed. He was, and the kids came. The older child, the one who got off the bus and said, "Mommy told me Tucker died," said several times over the course of the weekend, "It's so weird without Tucker here," or "Tucker usually follows us around when we play the game vacation," or "It is so quiet here without Tucker. I miss his schnozzle. Grammy, I think you should get another dog, but you should wait one week."

The younger child, the one who said we would see him again when we played vacation, is more pragmatic and has fewer filters. "Grammy, it is much easier coming into the house now. Tucker is not jumping on me. I still miss him, though."

The girls loved him. He left an impression on them. They knew he was part of the family. They knew how much David and I loved him.

It is one week shy of three months since I lost Tucker. When I take stock, as I did last week when I wrote about inventorying the positives in one's life, I realize I am slowly getting used to his absence. Slowly and with lots of setbacks. I still have this pounding realization that he is not here and I do not like it, but I am slowly letting that realization sink in. I read or saw something on one of the sites I post on that deals with pet loss or loss in general that struck me. It said something along the lines of the hole in your heart never goes away; it just stays there, and life grows around it. I believe that is true. My sadness that Tucker is not present to do what he used to do when the children were here is certainly there, but we still played vacation, we still did art projects, we still had a fashion show, we still baked—we lived; life goes on. We just did it without Tucker's nub wagging and his schnozzle schnozzling.

Tuesdays are generally busy days for me. I work a new part-time position. I leave relatively early and come back late in the afternoon. I pack up my things in the morning, I put away the coffee, I take out something for dinner to defrost, and I pick up my keys and leave. It is life, and it goes on, but what is different is that over the years, as a full-time teacher, Tucker had been conditioned (thank you, Pavlov) to the sound of my keys jingling. He always followed me down in the morning and stayed with me as I went through my morning routine, but as soon as he heard my keys, he would run back upstairs and jump back into the bed with David. I went to work, and Tucker went upstairs. I now go to work, and David remains upstairs alone.

At the risk of repeating myself, those of you who know, know how Tucker greeted me when I came home. Now I come home from work minus the canine fanfare. The human fanfare still exists and our fambily hugs are now just the two of us, not the three of us. Life goes on. We just do it without Tucker jumping up to join us in our hug, and I no longer get to say, "It's our little fambily." And that stings. It was one of my favorite things. One arm around David's waist and the other one wrapped around Tucker.

We don't stay up late and burn the midnight oil. We have a fairly standard nighttime routine. And if, for some reason, a late dinner, company, a good movie, or some other human distraction kept us busy, Tucker would begin to whine. He would jump off the couch and move out of the room, heading to the stairs. He would look back over his shoulder to see if we were following. He would let us know in no uncertain terms that it was time for the fambily to retire. And you know what? Most of the time, we would follow. If we did not, two things might occur. Tucker would go up by himself, or he would just plop down on the floor and wait for us, looking as miserable as he could until we acquiesced and moved upstairs. Well, we still keep a relatively early schedule, but sometimes we don't. We still climb the stairs and go up, but we do it quietly, under no canine pressure. We still have to go to sleep because life goes on. We just go upstairs without Tucker's collar jingle-jangling as he climbs the steps ahead of us.

When we went upstairs, we had a routine. The television was on *Law and Order*, or we read, or David would work on editing his photography. It was quiet and serene, and Tucker-Bean would sleep peacefully at the foot of the bed until David would start to sneeze. People sneeze, but when David sneezes, it is an avalanche. It is one sneeze after another, and it continues for a long enough period that you have to stop saying "God bless you" because you start to sound like a parrot. Nubby-Bean would hear the sneezes begin, and he would quickly move his position from the end of the bed up to the head of the bed. He would place his neck, face, and schnozzle across David's chest as if to protect him from, as my husband calls it, "the sneeze monster." Nubby-Bean would stay there, resting quietly, protecting his human papa until he was convinced the sneeze monster was gone. Then he would retreat to his place at the foot of the bed. Well, David still gets sneeze attacks, and when the only thing to protect him from the sneeze monster is the Kleenex, David's tears well. But people sneeze, and life goes on. He just wipes his nose without Tucker being there to protect him from the nasty sneeze monster.

I start planning Thanksgiving early. Thanksgiving is my

favorite holiday. I love reading cookbooks and dog-earing the pages of dishes I might like to try. It is an enjoyable time as I envision what colorful dishes and festive accouterments I will use. I have a lot of cookbooks that are housed in various locations. Whenever I got up from the table to go get another book, Tucker would stand up and follow me out. I wasn't going anywhere farther than four feet away, but he got up to follow me. When I came back into the room, he came back into the room. It was a warm feeling for me—this routine. I often cooked samples beforehand to see if the food actually tasted as good as those pictures looked. Tucker stood next to me by the kitchen island as I prepared food. Waiting, waiting, waiting, staring intently, waiting for me to drop something or to simply feed him whatever it is I am cooking.

I still read recipes and mark them. I still walk from room to room getting books, and his absence is palpable. I really miss his presence on the kitchen floor next to me as I generate a menu and drink coffee. But my family is coming, the food will be cooked, the desserts will be yummy, the children will decorate the house, and my ninety-nine-year-old father will preside over our What We Are Thankful For toasts, and life goes on. It will just go on without Tucky sitting next to me, waiting for me to drop a morsel of food on the floor.

And as life goes on, I get used to doing life without Tuck, but I also know I like life with a loyal, loving dog. I like it and I miss it. Tucky, you have been gone eleven weeks, and even though life goes on, it goes so differently. It goes on without your presence, without your kisses, and without your incessant begging for a cookie. So I will spirit you some cookies and spirit you, my love. Let me know if you are running out of blue racquetballs. I will throw them up and across the Rainbow Bridge. Rest well, my Nubby-Bean.

Life goes on, the hole remains, life goes on around it.

WEEK 12

Jealousy is a human emotion. People get jealous when they feel slighted or feel they deserve more. When you are jealous, you want something you do not have. You envy people who have it. Jealousy is a dark emotion. I suppose that being jealous can motivate you to work harder to get what you want or feel you justly deserve, but mostly, I think it hurts you and makes you less than the person you might know yourself to be. Jealousy or envy —and there is a dispute on whether those two words are actually synonyms—is draining. It washes away positive feelings and energy. How can you enjoy yourself if you are adrift in the sea of jealousy? Adrift in the pain of being unable to escape from your self-imposed prison of being a bottomless pit of need and want.

Imagine this: you get invited to a large party at a large house filled with beautiful people who have many beautiful things. All you do is look around at all those beautiful physical manifestations of wealth, and jealousy consumes you. "I want a house like this. I want that car. I want this, I want that, I want to have the latest and the greatest. Why them and not me? Why can't I?" And before you know it, it is time to leave, and instead of leaving feeling happy because you connected with people or feeling satisfied because you were laughing and enjoying yourself, you leave the house jealous, angry, and resentful. Are you better off? Those feelings don't go away. They stick to you like sap on your fingers, which is incredibly annoying and hard to get off. Jealousy immobilizes you. You become fossilized and stuck in your inability to move on.

Jealousy and envy are emotions we all share, but they are also emotions that we all hide and feel embarrassed about. No one really wants to admit they are jealous of someone else. It stabs at your sense of self-worth and value. Perhaps it points out some type of inferiority you are feeling. Who knows? It just makes you feel that "they are *better than* me." Maybe we should all be far more critical and more introspective about our own jealousies. Maybe we should really look at what is behind it all.

I read many posts about losing pets. I belong to no fewer than twelve grief sites. I pay very close attention to all the sites related to canine lymphoma. Those sites are particularly heartbreaking but also heartwarming places to be. That seems very oxymoronic. How could a site that tears your heart out and stomps on it also pick it up and elevate you to feeling the highest levels of support and love? I have mentioned before that when you have a dog afflicted with lymphoma, you die twice. Once when the diagnosis comes in and once again when you say goodbye. The canine lymphoma club is one you do not want to belong to. And that is because there is no happy ending.

Every family whose fur baby is diagnosed with that disease is facing a treacherous road ahead. The disease is fatal. It cannot be cured. That is a hard thing to come to terms with. It is scary to know that everyone on the lymphoma sites is on a timeline.

Where you place yourself on that timeline is dependent on how your dog reacts to treatment, how the disease is presenting, and the type of lymphoma your dog has. If you're lucky, you can stay at the remission line for a very long time. I found myself feeling jealous of all those happy stories of remission. Jealous of the posts that conveyed that remission had been achieved after only one dose. Jealous of all the posts that made me realize that I was not as lucky but I wanted to be. Jealous of all the happy family pictures. But what good did that jealousy do? Did it make me feel better? No, it did not. Would my jealousy have helped a fellow sufferer who was also undergoing a painful journey? No, it would not. So, what positives could come out of an emotion that serves no one? What exactly was I jealous of?

It comes with a price, you know. That jealousy. I was there. I know that once you get that diagnosis, your heart sinks and your whole world changes as you begin the treatment. Will it work, how will it affect him or her? Did I miss something? Was it my fault? As the days separated the treatments, I watched Tucker like a hawk, and when the day came to return to Cornell, I sat there in the waiting room, wondering what the vet was going to say when she came back in. I am not jealous of anyone who sits or paces while the chemo is being administered. I am not jealous of anyone who is being deafened by the clock ticking in his or her head, ticking off the days or weeks or minutes until the disease wins.

When I left the hospital, filled again with the knowledge that the protocol had failed, I was consumed with getting home and making sure that Tucker had a good afternoon. It was during the summer, so I let him swim. I was worried about knocking him out, and I did not want him to swim too much. I rationalized getting him out of the pool by telling myself that he did not know the difference between fifteen and ninety minutes, and as long as he had the chance to swim, he would be happy. He would sit and rest on the deck and I would watch him, the worry and sadness spreading through me. I was wondering about my misfortune and how I was going to get through this. I am not jealous of anyone who watches his or her dog lying on the floor or couch, chewing a ball or favorite toy and feeling sad at the realization that their time together is limited. I am not jealous of anyone who is going through that. I had a calendar to jot down everything I noticed. What his stools were like. What his appetite was like. What his mood was like. What his activity level was like. How fast it took him to settle down, wake up, and eat. No, I am not jealous of anyone who has to do that day in and day out.

And the pills. So many pills. The pill ingestion was the lifeline. I saw the distribution of those meds as the most important thing I had to do. My kitchen counter became a pharmacy. I had a schedule on the wall. I had the doggie version of a human pill container that holds the morning pills, the afternoon pills, the evening pills, and the emergency pills. What would I use to get those pills down? What would I do if nothing I hid the pill in worked? It seemed at times that Tucker would eat around the pill and spit the pill out. Or I would have to push it down his throat. I hated doing that. He was so trusting, and for me to have to hold open his mouth and push something down his throat and then hold his mouth closed until he swallowed made me miserable. I felt like I was betraying his trust. He looked to me for cookies and treats, freely given and freely consumed. "I am sorry, Nubby-Bean. I am sorry for having to stick my cold fingers down your throat to force this non-yummy tablet down your throat to try to keep you alive for one more day." Nope, I am not jealous of anyone who is forced to worry day in and day out about the medication. About its side effects. About keeping track of it. About watching it fail.

And, for certain, I am not jealous of anyone who is living with anticipatory grief.

So, I am going to shift the definition and shift the feeling. I am not jealous of anyone living with anticipatory grief. I feel for all of you. I feel for each of your heartbreaks. I feel all of your emptiness when you walk the floors at night because you cannot sleep. I feel how your gut aches when you wander your home in the wee hours of the morning. I feel all of your pain when you question when will I feel better, will I ever feel better, will the pain ever go away, why me? I feel all of your wishful thinking as you search and search and search for that perfect supplement, as you eliminate all the food you used to give him or her and start cooking cancer diets and hope beyond anything that it will help delay the inevitable.

And more than anything, instead of being jealous of anyone whose dog is in remission, I am going to say that I am thrilled and happy for all of you. Eat it up. Drink it up. Take it in because once it is gone—it is a huge hole. The hole that I wrote about last week. One of the biggest pieces of advice I got from many people, advice that I understood but had a hard time following, was trying to live in the moment. Dogs live in the present; they are in the present. I had a very hard time doing that, but that is not going to stop me from saying it was a good idea. Live in the moment, hold on to those kisses, and throw those balls because you never know when he or she will no longer be physically present.

Tucker, it has been twelve weeks, three whole months, but I no longer feel jealous of all those people who still have their beloved fur babies. I feel happy for them. And I feel grateful and happy that you blessed my life for eight beautiful years. And I still have all those memories, Bean. Lymphoma did not take those away from me. I win. Tucky, I hope you know how much David and I love you and miss you. I hope you know the joy you brought. I hope you know we will never ever throw away the container of blue racquetballs that I had hidden so that you could not smell them. They are not hidden now. They are out in the open. We'll play fetch, right? We'll play fetch when I get to the other side of the rainbow because somewhere over the rainbow is where you are.

Jealousy is a powerful and destructive emotion, yet it is one that affects everyone. My two granddaughters celebrate their birthdays within three weeks of each other. And even though they are involved with the parties and share the gifts, my older granddaughter pulled her mommy aside on the day of her younger sister's birthday and said, "I am feeling jealous." Good for her for being able to verbalize the emotion.

Jealousy is an emotion I felt often as a child and young teenager. I was jealous of my sister, who was more popular than I was. She had many friends, got invited to party after party, and seemed to be enjoying life in a way that I could not. I was jealous. There were girls who had long, straight hair; I did not. It was the time before flat irons, so wrapping your hair around your head was the route I had to take, and it very rarely worked. So I was jealous. There were other reasons to be jealous, but none as striking as the one I remember so clearly.

I had turned fifteen on November 6, and my birth mother, Julia, died at fifty-two on December 29, 1969. I was a teenage girl who was lost. I had no idea just how lost I was.

There are some things I remember, some things I don't. I remember being in California and coming home when we heard she had taken a turn for the worse. I remember hearing they found blood in her spinal cord. Don't remember what that meant. Do remember it wasn't good. Do remember going into the hospital room. Do remember what her face looked like. I'll never forget that. That look is etched in my brain like the finest ink on the tiniest scrimshaw. Don't remember how long I was there. Don't remember leaving the hospital. Don't remember getting home. Do remember sleeping in the basement. Do remember taking a sedative. Do remember my best friend calling me from Jamaica. She was on vacation with her family, and her mother had read the obituary in the *New York Times*. She told her daughter, "Call your friend, Sheila. Her mother died."

I vaguely remember talking to Anne. I remember coming upstairs from the basement area that we were sleeping in to talk. And then my dad came into the room and started to make the calls. There were no computers, Facebook, or social media. People were informed by phone. He sat cross-legged on the synthetic red carpet in a small alcove that led into the kitchen. Standing in the kitchen, I watched as he dialed the phone. Who the first call was to I do not remember, but I remember exactly what he said.

"Julia died last night."

And with those four words, the trajectory of my life changed.

Many of those days, weeks, and months following my mother's death are a blur. They were filled with adjustments. After she died and I returned to school, the ineffectual guidance counselor called me into his office to find out how I was doing. Some canned condolences, some routine "let me know if there is anything I can do for you" comments. Seemed so shallow. But all of a sudden, I found that I was on the receiving end of attention from many of the kids in school. Those girls. The ones I was so jealous of. The girls who did not know I was alive or even mattered before my mother died. The girls who never said hello when I walked past them in the hall. The girls who never invited me to parties or requested a playdate. The girls who never welcomed me at their lunch tables, and on the few occasions I was able to sit at the table, it was because I managed to secure the table first. The ones whom I wanted to be friends with were showering me with attention. I was thrilled, then. After all, they were the chosen ones. They were the ones I so desperately wanted.

There were no assigned seats in the cafeteria, but people tended to gravitate to the same table. I knew where the table I wanted to be at was, so I asked to leave class, slightly before the end, to use the restroom. I remained in the restroom until the bell rang and then rapidly took off for the cafeteria. I sat down at the table, and when I saw one of the girls enter, I said, "Hey, Jane, over here. I got the table already." She walked over. I don't remember what she said or if she said anything at all. When the next girl entered the cafeteria, I said it again: "Bonnie, over here. I got the table." The rest of the girls came over and sat down, and while no one kicked me out, no one acknowledged me, either.

But there was something lacking. Yes, I was sitting at the table with the girls with straight hair. I was sitting at the table with all the girls I was jealous of, but I could have been in Kansas. Being at the table did not matter. I felt like Hester Prynne. She was shunned from her community, and I was shunned from the lunch conversation.

"It was a great party, wasn't it?"

"Yeah, and I bet the one on Saturday will be just as good."

"My mom said she would drive us, okay?"

Imagine listening to that. No invitation was given to me. It did not matter if I was at the table, and in fact, it was worse because, in addition to omitting me, they were also taking advantage of me. When I look back on this experience now, I still feel the humiliation and the desperation. It is softened now and doesn't bite as much, but it is much like grief that mellows but never goes away.

As I sat there eating my lunch, chewing on whatever it was that tasted like dust, I heard Bonnie say she wanted to get a container of milk. "I'll get you one," I said, jumping up so quickly I nearly tripped over my chair.

"Ah, yeah, sure," she said. I am not sure what transpired at the table when I got up to leave because my back was toward the girls, but I am fairly certain they were not singing my praises. When I returned to the table and placed the milk container next to her, I noticed there was something missing from my own lunch tray. My Ring Ding. I did not buy lunch often. It did not have anything to do with money but because I liked bringing lunch. Perhaps one of the reasons I did like bringing lunch was because there was, as I remember, a stash of good snack foods at home. I have some very vivid memories of the snack foods we had.

When I was sick, one of the snack foods that my mother often gave me was Drake's Raisin Cakes. These were large, round, moist yellow cakes that were dense and filled with raisins. The cake itself was honey-sweet, and the chewy raisins left such a sweet taste in my mouth. I have vivid memories of that cake, and I have been trying to find it again. My sister remembered them, too. She even reached out to Drake's to inquire about them. They said they never made a cake like that, but we both know they did.

Of course, we were not limited to eating that cake only when sick, but I do remember always having it when I was sick. I suppose it didn't make the list of top ten cake choices because there was no chocolate. And what self-respecting child would choose raisins over white artificial cream, but it was their loss. But Ring Dings were something else. Now, they still make them, but they are not the same. They are smaller and the chocolate is bitter. The chocolate coating is thinner than it used to be, and it cracks. When you put it in your mouth, you are eating wax. The cake is dry and holey, and the cream center is a major disappointment. Not earth-shattering, but, well, actually, it is an earth-shattering disappointment when you have the 1960s version tattooed in your long-term memory.

The Ring Ding that graced my lunch box was the vintage model. One large, round, shiny, chocolate-glazed treat that was stuffed full of sweet white cream that burst into your mouth when you bit into it. The cake was smooth and sweet, the chocolate melted in your mouth, it did not taste like wax, and it was missing.

When I sat down and noticed the missing treat, I knew someone had taken it. "Who took my Ring Ding?" Silence all around. I asked again. No answer.

Now, here is where memory tricks you. I truly do not remember if anyone confessed, but I do seem to remember that I accused one girl—Bonnie. Maybe she snottily said, "I did." And maybe she didn't, but no one seemed to care, and that is when I realized that no matter what I did, no matter how often I tried, no matter how often I prostituted myself to try to get them to like me, it was not going to happen. I believe I left the cafeteria table and the cafeteria itself without saying a word.

But after my mother died, these girls reached out to me and sat with me and invited me over, and all of a sudden, I was accepted. I had something to do after school. There were phone calls. I was happy, but it did not last. I do not know how long the faux friendship went on for, I do not know how long I felt happy, but I do remember that I once said to myself that if it took my mom to die to be popular, it was worth it. I am not sure if I had that thought more than once, and I am pretty sure that I never told anyone that, and I am pretty sure that I am still having a hard time admitting that I had that feeling. How very sad that I had such little self-assurance or confidence that I would sell the memory of my mother in order to feel connected. Would I have felt the same way if I had felt more at ease with my relationship with my mother? I don't know, but I can see now how lost and lonely I must have been to believe in the inauthenticity of the girls who were merely expressing pity and how I could possibly determine that the death of a loved one was worth the shallow pity that was coming my way. And yes, it was jealousy that led me to behave in such a pitiful manner.

As time passed, I found a wonderful friend, Anne, the girl who called me from Jamaica. We were so close that we did everything together. We were always on the phone. She came into my life and filled my days with fun and friendship. My jealousy of those other girls subsided. Anne had a fun household. She had a brother, a sister, and a big, funny dog named George. We had many sleepovers and spent a lot of time listening to the Allman Brothers and Traffic. I liked being at her house. Her mom was really nice and was always very nice to me.

My mom had been deceased for a while, but I am not quite sure how long. We had had a series of housekeepers who tried to keep the house going. People who cleaned and cooked, but none of whom were actually effective moms. I spent a lot of time at Anne's house. I believe we were upstairs in her room when her mom called us down for dinner. Maybe lunch? I remember that Anne did not respond. Her mom called again, her voice noticeably more annoyed. Again, Anne made no comment. A third request.

"Anne, your mom is calling us down."

"So."

"Anne!"

I felt myself reaching a fever-pitched anger at her. How could she ignore her mother? How could she sit there sifting through her albums, trying to decide which one to play, while her mother was downstairs yelling for us to come down? How could she possibly treat her mother like that?

"Anne! I can't believe you are ignoring her. What is wrong with you? Don't you get it? Don't you realize how lucky you are?"

By this time, my anger and jealousy were bubbling out of control. And I was crying. I had to go home. There was no way I could stay overnight in her house.

"Daddy, come get me."

I don't remember what Anne said. I don't remember what her mom said. But I had to get out of that house. I was so jealous that she had a mom and

I did not. I simply could not remain in a home where the mom was being treated so poorly. I don't really think she understood my outburst. I don't think she felt she deserved the rage that was thrown at her. I don't think she understood my desperate need to escape. But I also don't think she understood the level of my grief and the enormity of my jealousy. How could she possibly understand what it was like to be fifteen, motherless, angry, and lost? And if you haven't been there, consider yourself lucky.

WEEK 13

I am almost at a loss for words, which is very unusual for me. I usually have too many words. Anatomically, my dentists have told me that it is hard to get into the back of my mouth because my mouth is small, but that is totally unrelated to my usual verbosity. But I am slightly at a loss for what to say. I have talked about loss—although that is not a closed topic. I have talked about guilt—and I still feel good that I do not feel guilty for any decisions I've made. I have talked about jealousy and still believe that being jealous is a waste of energy. So what is left? I have talked about the idea that I don't think my loss will ever go away, even as I learn to live with it. I still think about Tucker every day. I miss him so much. I look at pictures, and I want him back. I see videos that sting when I watch him run and chase balls. And I wonder when the pain will go away.

I have seen many posts about seeing signs and animal communicators. If that works for fellow sufferers, I am happy. I am happy for anything that helps anyone cope with the loss. In a recent *Time* magazine that was devoted to dogs and their importance to humans, the history of domestication was outlined. Dogs and humans have been building a connection for tens of thousands of years. Ancient art, way before the Christian

Era, depicts how important dogs were to civilizations. With tens of thousands of years binding us to dogs, it is no wonder that we are so devastated when they depart. I don't really believe in signs, but I do believe that seeing things that trigger your memory is a way of bringing your beloved back to your conscious mind. In that respect, it is a sign.

You look up at the sky and see a cloud shaped like your dog bending down with his mouth open. It reminds you of his favorite play position. You take a walk, and the wind blows a stick in front of you. It looks like the sticks your dog would bring to the door. It reminds you of all the times you played fetch. A squirrel runs by, and you hear his bark echoing in the corners of your mind. You remember the pull on the leash as he tried to get that squirrel. Not really signs, but triggered memories that remind you not only of your loss but also of the joy you experienced.

How else does one remember? How do the memories of your baby change over time? Do they become clearer, or do they fade? I am glad that my memories are as vivid as they are. I am glad that I haven't forgotten anything. There is one thing that many people do that I want to do but have not yet done. To shrine or not to shrine? That is the question. I read so many posts from people who create these beautiful physical memorials to their lost pets. I have read many posts from people who, like me, want to but can't. I know there is no timeline, but I can't do it yet. But just because I can't, doesn't mean I haven't started collecting, literally collecting physical things.

I have sympathy cards that I have saved. I have a rainbow candle. David found an unfinished bone in the closet. I have a dish towel with a Boykin picture on it. I have a Boykin statue. I have individually framed photos and a wall photo collage. I have a beautiful stained-glass window hanging being made for me; I have a beautiful urn being made for me. I have his portrait, I have his leash, I have his collar. I have a whole container of unused blue racquetballs that he never got to play with. I have a bowl of blue racquetballs that I gathered from the yard that he did play with. I have a Boykin sweatshirt, a beautiful birthday gift from David, and I have Boykin shirts. I also have two Cuddle Clones. I saw many ads for this product on Facebook, with videos of people opening the packages and hugging the animals. They all cried. Every time I saw an ad, I broke down both in tears and in my decision to buy one, then two.

    The people who work for the company are so nice. You send pictures and you fill out information about your pet. One of the questions they ask is whether or not the animal is deceased. They are very communicative and seem very dedicated to their product and to the customer. A percentage of the proceeds go to feeding animals in rescue. The Clones arrived several weeks ago. I have not opened them yet. Why? I am afraid they will look so much like Tucker that I will break down. I am afraid they will look so much like him that when I realize it really isn't him, I will say to myself, "Who am I kidding? Was I really thinking that a stuffed animal, even if it looks like Tucker, is going to make the hole smaller? Take away the truth? Wake me up from a dream that I never signed on for? Or am I afraid that it won't look anything like Tucker, dashing my hopes that its likeness will be just like having him back with me?" The packages sit in the corner of the room, just like his ashes and his paw print that still sit in the bag I retrieved from the hospital: on the shelf, in the room where I placed them when we brought him home.

The artist who is making the stained glass for me says she will create a cabochon for me, and she will scatter some of Tucker's ashes into the glass creation. But that would mean that I have to find the courage to open up the box of his remains, and I can't, not yet. So, for all of you who have created these beautiful memorials, and I know you are many, how has it helped? Do you feel comforted when you pass by that designated area? Do you stop in front of it and meditate? Do you find yourself walking a different way because it is too painful to see your creation? I know I will create something that will attempt to do justice to the love I have for Tucker. Thirteen weeks in, I simply want to say that I understand how unique and different we all are as we cope with the loss we all feel. I understand that as life continues to unfold, I will continue to live it to my fullest and to the best of my ability. Tucker taught me to grasp the positives and enjoy the joy. His ever-wagging nub of a tail was a sure sign of his happiness. His ability to find happiness in a simple blue racquetball is a strong lesson to find that simplicity and to relish in the small pieces of light and happiness when I can.

It is easy to forget that sometimes, but it is a good lesson. Find the joy in the memories, and when those triggers or signs come, smile, hold on to them, and smile again. Nubby-Bean, I miss you, and I know the life we had with you was a good one. Thirteen weeks, Lemon-Head. Run free.

Love, Mama

WEEK 14

We are taking care of my husband's son's dogs, Jack and Rose. Two very loving dogs that we care for frequently. They played with Tucker, and they were friends. They know the house well. They know the term *outside*, and they know where to go. Jack is a good boy. He is getting older and is starting to have some health issues. Rose is a playful dog and will do anything for food and hugs. I call her a love bandit. I do not know if they realize Tucker is missing. One evening, when I let them outside, they were sitting on the deck. Jack was sitting in the same position Tucker would sit in. When I went to let them in, Jack's position looked so much like Tucker in the dusky light, I gasped. When they came inside, David gave them a treat. He said, "Do you want a cookie?" I was cooking and looked up at him with a tear welling in my eye, the same way it is welling as I write, and I said to him, "You sound exactly the same way you sounded whenever you asked if Tucker wanted a cookie."

Tucker, I wanted to give you a cookie. I wanted to give you a hug. I wanted to give you a kiss, but instead I am giving you this poem, from my heart.

Recipe For a Life with Tucker

Take a few pounds of chocolate fuzzy fur that sits in your lap with large, imploring eyes when you pick him up to bring him to his furever home.

Shower him with a reciprocal look that says, "Welcome home, little brown package of love. You have already captured our hearts, and we will do everything we can to love you and make you happy."

Stir in the dreams for a lifetime of hope and joy, love and devotion, trust and bonding, all topped off with a little pink tongue that feels soft and velvety on your skin.

Knead in Wubba toys that get chewed up, the blue racquetballs that become his signature trademark, and bones that get dragged outside and hidden away. The bones that you will find are buried in the backyard under his favorite clump of grass long after he has gone away and can no longer chew them. The bone that now sits on the counter with teeth marks and ragged edges. The bone that you would give anything for if you could just say, "Tucker, you want a bone?" one more time.

Mix in large buckets of tender loving care as the little brown swamp poodle learns to love his home and his humans as this brand-new family forms. Make sure there are extra servings of tender loving care when the thunder rumbles, and the nub goes between his legs and he shakes and jumps on your lap.

Whisk in an infinite number of cuddles, kisses, hugs—and that is from the hoomans.

Stir it all together.

Sift in your infinite infatuation with that cute brown nose that matches his fur, that feels so wet and tickly when he rubs his face in yours. Don't forget to fall in love with that muss on top, that all-too-perfect topknot the groomers love and style when they see him.

Measure out a fair amount of discipline, so the best Boykin does not become the best Destroykin. Make sure that all your socks are accounted for so the sock is found in your drawer and not on the X-ray of his GI tract.

Pepper that discipline with treats and soften it with long walks filled with aromas and scents that set that little nub off wagging.

Let sit at room temperature on your bed with his head on your lap for several years. Then mix in the cuteness overload when you tell him to "high five," and he lifts his front paws to touch your hand. Be neat and don't forget to wipe the tears when you see the empty space at the end of the bed.

Grate and add the hours and hours and hours of tireless ball chasing. Whisk in his joy and your smiles. Don't forget to fold in the swimming and his endless shaking as he tirelessly jumps in the pool to retrieve that ball.

Separate out the worry when the diagnosis comes in and put it into a bowl, cover it with a soft cloth dampened by your tears, and try harder than you ever thought you could to live for the moment and grab the gifts of one more day for as long as you have them.

Slice and dice every single memory you have and cement them permanently in your mind. Bake those memories until done, and make sure you package them carefully so you can access them when your heart shakes and your mornings are too quiet.

Take them out and place those memories at the forefront of your mind.

Taste them. Let the sweetness spread through you. Let it linger. And just remember the grief you taste now is because of the love you had before.

Serving Size: The best LBD. (Little Brown Dog. Just one of the many nicknames that Boykins have.) The best life with Tucker Nubby-Bean. It has been fourteen weeks since you have left. Thanksgiving is coming. Your friends will be here, as always, hanging out in the kitchen, waiting for a dropped morsel. I will miss you, my Tucky boy; I will miss you hanging out with me in the kitchen.

Remember that love grows and that one day you will realize you are so smitten with that little brown dog that you can't imagine ever having lived without him before he joined your world and can't imagine ever living without him again now that he is gone.

In the time that has elapsed between writing my many thoughts and this book being published, Jack has passed. Jack, a beloved pet in our family, was a wonderful friend. He was loved by everyone, and he loved Tucker. He was a city dog who loved his visits here so that he could run outside and sit outside for hours. He would sit outside and view the world, and when many of the other dogs would come inside, Jack would stay. Jack, you are missed, and I hope you are running wild and free up there with Tucker.

WEEK 15

Hi. This is me, Tucker. I have to get in here to let you know what I know and see. I have been watching with love what my mama does every day and what she writes each week. And now it is time for me to talk to her.

Mama, I watch you cry into your pillow at night as you move your legs around, hoping to feel my body stopping you from stretching your legs out completely. I watch you every morning, early. You always got up early, and I would always follow you downstairs, even if I thought it was too early. I watch you every morning when you go to your desk and see that the first thing you do is look at my portrait and touch my green collar. I loved that collar. I am glad you did not throw that collar out. I hope when you touch that collar, you feel me next to you. I am here, Mama. Every time you touch that collar, you are touching me. And those pictures you have all around the house. It makes me so happy to see them. There are so many I love. Like the one you have of me trotting toward you, carrying my ball. My blue racquetball. Do you know there are so many racquetballs where I am? I will never run out; I will never have to whine near the bathroom door again. I know that is where you hid them. I know that; I always knew that. I just didn't want you to know I knew because I wanted you to think you were surprising me with a new ball. I always liked how excited you looked when you gave me the ball.

I notice many other pictures, too. I see how you linger on the one of me where you are laughing and I am sitting up on the chair with you. I remember the time that picture was snapped. I don't remember what was said that made you laugh because I only speak dog, but I do know it must have been funny because you laughed. I loved it when you laughed because I knew you were happy. Mama, try to keep laughing, okay? I want you to laugh because I love you. I am not sad that you and Dad let me go because I was not really myself anymore, and it was getting hard for me to breathe. You know what I like when I look down and see you? I like the fact that you still talk about me. I like the fact that you think of me and I am still there. I know you still grieve, Mama. I know it hits you at different times and sometimes it comes on so suddenly. Like the time you were driving and saw someone walking a dog. I think it was a springer spaniel. He really did look like me. Even I had to look twice. I saw how you had to pull over to the side of the road. You put your head on the steering wheel and sobbed. I saw that, and I wished I could have come to you to lick your face. You always did like that. It was so funny when I would get into the licking mode. You would be sitting on the floor and Lilah and Nani would be at the table begging you to make me dance, or high five, or walk backward for a treat. And then they would laugh. Everyone was having a good time watching me and it made me happy, so I would just come over and schnozzle you.

You know, I always knew the girls made that word up. Schnozzle means "kiss," and when I came over to you, I just couldn't stop schnozzling. You could hardly come up for air. Those were good times, Mama. Keep thinking about that and you will be happy. I promise. I know how hard it is for you now that I am gone. I do. I also know the time we had together was the best time any little brown dog could have ever had. I cherished every time we played and went swimming. I cherished every time we went for a walk. I am sorry if I never got that down. I know you tried really hard to train me, but every time I smelled a smell or saw something move, I couldn't help myself. I ended up walking you instead. Do you forgive me, Mama? I still liked the walks.

You know what else I want to tell you? I want to talk about my bones. Oh, I did so love the many bones we had. The marrow bones were the best. I could smell them as soon as you pulled up in the driveway. You would take them out of the grocery bag, and in that high-pitched voice you used only when you were talking to me, you would say, "Oooooh, look what I have. Look here," and I would know, and I would come closer to you and sit down and stare up at you with those puppy dog eyes I never lost and wait patiently. And you would say, "I have a bone for you. A special bone," and out the package would come. You would tear off the plastic and hand me the meatiest, most delicious bone that ever existed and I would take it to my special place. Oh, those were good times and good bones. I buried them, you know. Bailey, my friend Bailey the beagle, was the only one who could smell where they were. I saw you a few days ago when Dad came into the room and gave you a bone he found in the closet, I think. Yeah, I hid them everywhere. I see that you did not throw it out. I know you kept it because it was my bone. I see that you have a lot of my things. I am so glad. Mama, I see the blue racquetballs. The ones on your shelf will always be my favorite because those are the ones that you and Dad threw for me in the pool and in the yard, and those were the ones that, even when I wanted to bark, I wouldn't drop the ball out of my mouth. Wasn't that a funny sound I made, my muffled bark, when I had the ball in my mouth? You always laughed. That made me happy. I would drop the ball and come to lick your face, and then I would get a cookie. I see you, Mama, shedding a tear as you write this. Please, don't be sad. Those times were the best. Smile when you think of them.

Mama, it is amazing to me how connected we were. I am pretty sure you knew exactly what I wanted and exactly what I needed. When I was scared, you called me up to your lap. When I was getting sicker, I saw and knew that you were worried. I knew that every walk we took, every game we played, every cookie I got was given to me out of love. I want you to know I knew that you would never do anything to hurt me. And I also knew that on that last day, the evening when I could not settle down and the oxygen wasn't helping me, I knew that you would help me pass quietly. I want to let you know that it was okay, and I am glad that you did not leave me alone in that back area of Cornell Hospital. I didn't really know what was going on, but it wasn't home and I am glad you were there. I don't remember much, but I do remember when I started to feel tired, and Mama, I felt your hands on me, and it felt good. It felt like love, Mama. You helped me cross. Mama, I know it is fifteen weeks now. I know it has been the hardest fifteen weeks you have ever spent. But please try to cry tears of love and celebrate what we had instead of what we did not. I will chase the balls, and I will come to you in your dreams. And on this Thanksgiving weekend, be grateful. I know I am grateful that you were my whole life for the eight beautiful years we had.

Love, your Nubby-Bean, Lemon-Head.

WEEK 16

Good morning, Tucky. I am so happy you reached out. How did you know I was longing to hear from you? And of course, you must know I am writing to you now and it is very early in the morning. And, yes, I do touch the collar. Tucker, as long as it is quiet now, I will try to fill you in on all that has happened in the four months since you left me. You know, Tucker, truth be told, and don't take this the wrong way, sometimes I just can't believe you left me. I know, I know, it does not make sense, and you did not do it on purpose. I know you would have stayed longer to play and love, but at times, I am still in shock when I come downstairs alone. I never put my needs in front of yours, especially when you were having trouble breathing and living your best life, but damn it, I miss you. I am not sure you will understand this and I am not sure that this makes sense, but sometimes it feels easier to deal with your absence, yet it isn't easier at all. Ugh, I do not know how to explain it.

Since you left, little Lilah lost her first tooth. Lilah, you remember her, right? She used to be worried that you would jump up on her when she came to visit, so she would hide behind her dad's legs for a few minutes. Well, she lost her first tooth, and she was so proud of herself. When she came here for Thanksgiving, she couldn't stop sticking her tongue through the hole in her mouth. She thought that was so funny. And her sister, Nani, well, she is just getting so big, Nubby-Bean. Yesterday, she told me that she really misses you, especially during a bath. Nubby-Bean, this is what she said,

"Grammy, it was always so much fun to take a bath at your house, and I really thought it was funny when Tucky would come in and stick his schnozzle in the water and drink it. And then he would have bubbles on his nose."

Nubby-Bean, I miss that, too. It just shows what I mean about missing you. The girls still take a bath here. They still play in the water. They still use bubbles, but you are not running upstairs the minute you hear the squeaking of the pipes that you knew was the bath water. It is your absence in everyday things that is still so painful. Tucky, do you know what I mean?

Let's see. We made it through Thanksgiving. GiGi was here. Tucker-Bean. GiGi turned ninety-eight years old a few weeks after you crossed the bridge. He was the one who had your portrait made. The beautiful portrait you see me touching and looking at every morning. Well, he looked at it on Thanksgiving and also at the beautiful flag that was made for me by a Boykin Nation member, and he shed a tear and said, "You know, when I come here, and I see all of Tucker's things, I think about Tucker, and you know, I feel the sadness that he is gone." He is ninety-eight years old, Tucky, and you touched him like you touched all of us.

You know, this morning, I was shaking out the laundry, Tucker, and separating those dang fitted sheets from everything else. When you wrote to me last week, you mentioned how you knew that losing you and the grief sometimes comes to me suddenly and unexpectedly. YOU KNEW THAT. Well, it happened again. Remember how when I shook the sheets and put them on the floor, you would run and plop down onto the sheet and then I had to get you off? Well, this morning, I shook the sheets, put them on the floor, and was simply able to pick them up and place them in the washing machine. I did not have to bend down to give you a little tickle on your topknot or a scratch under the chin or a gentle push off the sheet. "Tucky—get off the sheet." I did not have to do those things or say that, but I wanted to and still want to.

I wonder and continue to think about the truth of grief. It does not go away. It stays, but it just gets built into daily life. For example, I am in the grocery store and I am waiting in line and boom: I realize that I am not buying any marrow bones for you and I get sad. Or I pass by the fresh meat section, and I remember when I was making you a fresh cancer diet. I always bought the freshest of ingredients. Every time I pass that section, I think of you and how I was doing everything possible to help stave off your cancer—but you—you just enjoyed the food. To you, it was a great and delicious meal, and I could tell how happy you were when you saw the bowl. And that is how I want to remember your mealtime.

Nubby-Bean, the Dot was here over Thanksgiving. She is so cute, and she is much more comfortable here now. She jumps up on the couch where you used to sit, and she will lie down in Tucky-bed. She still will give the side-eye once in a while, but basically, she has learned to trust people again. The Dotticles would love to tell you that if she could.

Well, yesterday, I was with Nani and Lilah, and during homework time, we were talking about you, as usual. Well, during homework time, the girls earn Grammy points. Do you know what those are? I will tell you. They earn points for doing their homework and their reading, and then at some point (more frequently than necessary, but I am a grammy), they get little prizes when they turn in their points. Well, Lilah is in kindergarten and she doesn't have so much homework, so she draws pictures. We all worked on a picture together, and it was of you! I will show you a picture of it after I write this letter. I loved it so much I went and framed it, and it is now right underneath your beautiful portrait, Bean. So, truly, I am surrounded by you. And when you take a look, make sure you notice how the girls made your green collar!

Lemon-Head, it is four months since David and I came home from Cornell Hospital alone. It has been four months since we sat outside on the deck, realizing that you would never again go bounding down those stairs to get to the pool or run out to the fence—to the back forty, as we called it. Tucker, it has been four months since we held you and said how much we love you. Four months since we were a fambily of three, but in our hearts, we will always be that fambily. I love you, Bean. You are my one-and-only Nubby.

October 12

I suppose that if I can write to my Nubby-Bean, maybe it is time to write a letter to my mom, Julia.

Dear Mom,

I am a full-grown woman now, Mom, with children and grandchildren of my own. I don't really know where the years went. One day, I was playing hopscotch and the next, I was welcoming my first granddaughter. I am sure you would have loved being here to see that. If I could talk to you, there are so many things I would say. I would have to tell you that I do know you loved me, but I would also tell you that I felt you never understood who I was. On some level, I was always striving to get your attention and to get you to see me. I always felt that I could never compete with Debbie, who, as my younger sister, seemed to get more attention. Younger siblings often get more attention, but this was different. There appeared to me some deeper sense of connection between the two of you that I could never bridge.

In long discussions I have had with Daddy, he admits that my feelings about that were true. He did say that he believed there was a stronger connection between you and Debbie. It both stung and felt good when he said that. Why? Because there was some closure, some validation that all those feelings I had were not simply made up but were, in fact, based on truth. It no longer was crazy-making. But I also laughed when he told me that your philosophy on child-rearing was one of "benign neglect." As a mom, I now understand that!

I became a teacher, Mom. I floundered around with a variety of jobs for many years until I found myself in the school system. And I know how important a good education is to you. It was what motivated you to go back to work so that you and Daddy could pay for a private school in a town with better schools. I know how much you did not like how the New York City schools were being run and the many letters you wrote to the Board of Education complaining about the quality of the schools. I am sure you would have been very proud of the work I did in the more than two decades I taught.

Mom, I had a pretty hard time growing up. I guess I always felt a little like a misfit in the family. I knew you had a deep connection with Deah—well, Debbie. She changed her name when she got older. I was jealous of that. But I know now, as an adult, that you did the best you could. Here is what age and wisdom do. I was, truth be told, Mom, a little embarrassed about you when I was in my early teens. You did not look the part. You were a true bohemian in your appearance. And oh, how I appreciate that now. You wore handmade embroidered overalls. It wasn't a common type of attire for moms in the late sixties. The hippie movement of different types of clothes was just starting, but for people a good deal younger. Most moms in the neighborhood were more conventionally dressed. It made me uncomfortable, but now I can see just how creative you were and how you clearly marched to your own beat.

I will tell you something else, Mom. I am so happy to say that I still have a box of your writings. I have many of the Giant Step Awards and the many stick-figure letters you wrote to me to calm my nerves and fears when I was little. I always appreciated them. And while I do question whether those stories were another manifestation of your creativity, or whether they were the only way you felt you could communicate with me, I am so happy and proud to have them. I read them the other day for the first time in over fifty years, and they were wonderful.

    I ended up being a pretty creative individual, Mommy, and I like to write. I like to write all types of things, but I am really enjoying writing picture books for kids. And I got that from you! So, despite the feelings of despair, anger, and confusion that I have harbored about you over the decades that you have been gone, I am telling you that I am also harboring respect, gratitude, and love.

    Love,
    Sheila

WEEK 17

I have been thinking a lot about suffering. Suffering is a human condition. It is such a part of the human condition that scholars and theologians have been pontificating over human suffering for thousands of years. I am not a theologian, and if I have omitted an important belief or if I made an error, I ask for forgiveness. It was not intentional.

All major religions have something to say about suffering. No one wants to suffer, yet it is something we all do. Muslim belief sees suffering as a part of Allah's plan for human beings. It is believed that suffering will make one stronger and that suffering should be expected and accepted because there will be a reward in the next life. The Christian faith views suffering as a natural consequence of sin, and it exists because we live in a broken world. Evil and suffering are seen as a preparation for heaven, since it gives people an opportunity to become better and improve their souls. Jews see the concept of reward and punishment as an explanation for the existence of suffering. The covenant between God and the people of Israel elaborates that suffering will be visited upon those who abandon the ways of God. Buddhists believe that desire and ignorance are the roots of suffering. Craving pleasure, material goods, and immortality are all unattainable, and as a result, craving them can only bring suffering. Hinduism views suffering as part of life. It is part of the world in which we live, and accepting suffering allows people to move forward.

Whatever the great religions' views are on suffering, I will tell you what my view is. Suffering is pain. Suffering is a wound that reminds you of something difficult and painful that you are enduring. Suffering can make you feel lonely and isolated, but it is also a pain that can strengthen your convictions or change your way of thinking. It can allow empathy. For anyone who is suffering the loss of a loved one, I recognize your suffering and feel it intensely. For every post that recounts chemo's side effects and the bellyaches and the pacing and labored breathing you are witnessing in your furry friends, I suffer with you. No one wants to suffer; I would prefer not to do it, yet I would take it if it meant saving someone I love from its strangling tentacles.

As it relates to my grief journey, I still suffer, seventeen weeks in. I miss Tucker and the life we had with him because he was so much a part of our world. WE were three. I miss his cheerful presence and his quirks. All dogs have lovable quirks, but the Boykin quirks—like the sprawl and the never-ending need to swim and hold a ball—made Tucker who he was. I miss him. I miss how he sat outside the shower door, waiting for me to get out so that he could lick the water off my legs. I tried to stop that behavior but lost. I miss his whining when the ball rolled under the couch and it was just out of reach. How he would just sit splayed out on the floor looking at it. His whine was so pathetic I would stop whatever I was doing to bend down to get it, only to have to do it again a second later when he pushed it back under. There are so many things I miss, but I am learning—emphasis on *learning*—that life continues. So this is what I have to say about the march of life.

That's Life; It's What I Do.

> I baked a triple chocolate cake with fudge icing and mousse filling covered with cookie crumbs and a side of whipped cream.
> I read a book and discussed why I did not like it with a group of people I had never met on an internet book club filled with retired teachers.
> I have had multiple Facebook marketplace scammers try to engage me in conversation. Can't you find a better place to talk to someone instead of on a site that is for selling or buying items? I guess I am old because I don't understand why it is a thing to strike up conversations with someone who is trying to sell something. It is not a dating site. Either buy the item or not. Otherwise, don't talk to me.
> I read several cookbooks looking for recipes that I will probably never cook, yet I keep subscribing to Food Network magazine because there is nothing better than flipping those pages and marking them. Truth be told, the triple chocolate cake I referred to was from the magazine.
> I did all of that because that is what I do. That is life.

I went to work and helped a class of underserved children feel less underserved.

I wrote to my favorite author to tell her more about Tucker and to tell her what an inspiration she is in my own pursuit of becoming an author.

I visited my ninety-eight-year-old dad, who had to go to the doctor, so I took him because he does not drive and because he took care of me my whole life and I want to do the same.

I comforted several of my children; well, I tried to comfort several of my children who are having their own difficulties with being parents and worrying about their children.

I kissed my husband because I love him.

I did all of that because that is what I do. That is life.

I did all those things, but I did them without you, Tucker.

I liked watching *Law and Order* and mindlessly stroking under your neck, which was nice and smooth—before your swollen lymph nodes made their ugly and unwelcome appearance.

I went grocery shopping and wondered why I hadn't had a tasty piece of fruit in like forever, and why is a box of cereal over seven dollars, and what the hell is a jackfruit?

I took a walk and tried to relax. Sometimes I can, but sometimes I can't. It is a crapshoot; I never know which one it is going to be.

I cried. I cry a lot, but this time, I cried for my human family members who are struggling.

I woke up at 4 a.m. thinking that maybe, just

maybe, I would be able to go back to sleep but ended up sitting at the table drinking the first cup of coffee at 4:15 a.m. 4 a.m. is the new 9. By the time 9 a.m. actually rolled around, I had done the laundry, cleaned the refrigerator, prepared what I was going to make for dinner, and made a batch of coconut macaroons.

I brought my car in again to fill the tires with air because there was a slow leak, and while I was there, I filled the car with gas and remembered when full-serve was actually a thing.

I went to CVS to pick up a prescription they did not have because there was a shortage. I did all of that because that is what I do. That is life.

I just did it without you, Tucker, waiting for me at the door and jumping up with a squeal when I walked in and sat down to greet you. I did it without you disappearing momentarily into the other room to get that blue racquetball, your message that it was now time to play because I was home.

I started thinking about all the upcoming birthdays and celebrations and where to go and what to do and what would be a meaningful gift —knowing that the most meaningful gifts at this point cannot be found in stores or on Amazon. They can only come from the part of your heart that longs to give and help and love.

I made plans to have lunch with a friend, but it got canceled.

I talked to my sisters, my two besties, about our dad and politics and sickness and our combined lack of sleep.

I wondered why the world seemed so sad and angry.

I cleaned the closets but still could not part with much, even if the clothes had not been worn for maybe eight years.

I thought about how, despite my troubles, I am still fortunate to have people I love.

I did all of that because that is what I do. That is life.

I just did it without you, Tucker, sitting at attention, staring at the door, that low guttural sound emanating from your throat because you hear something that we can't hear. "What is it, Tucky? What do you hear? Is it making you nervous?" And I get up to see what I can't see or hear.

I do my life without my little brown dog, without my swamp poodle, without my Nubby- Bean. I don't think I will ever get over losing my good boy because I never knew the bond could be so strong. I never knew dogs get cancer. I always just assumed Tucker would live a really long life like all the other dogs in my family. I just never knew a dog could take up so much real estate in my heart and soul. It is hard to believe how much it still hurts and how the tears just come so suddenly. And for those of you who might not really be able to understand the constant the palpable hardness of grief, the attacks of despair, the loneliness in the morning, and the sadness of looking at a collar hanging on the wall, you are really lucky.

Hey, Bean. I hope you have met up with Buford, Dexter,

Molly, and the Chelse. I hope you are all frolicking around over that bridge and having the time of your lives!
    Mama

WEEK 18

I just have questions. It is early, as usual. I am sitting at my desk next to Tucker's portrait and his collar. I touch his collar, and I look at the portrait like I do every morning. It is painted with pastel chalk so the colors are muted, and when you look closely at it, you can see how the pastel particles create a pillowy softness to the portrait. A softness that matches the feathery furriness of Tucker's coat. And I ask *why*? Why can't I tussle your fur? Why can't I scratch your topknot?

I am no stranger to death. I lost two women in my life. My mother and my stepmother, whom I refer to as my moms. Two wonderful women who gave so much to me. I know time eases the sudden pangs of pain. I know time allows you to slowly integrate what you miss into your own life. I know time allows reflection. My birth mother, Julia, was a creative woman who wrote beautifully. She had a unique way of dealing with her children's troubles. She was, indeed, quirky. I inherited that. And I appreciate that.

Trudy, my stepmom, with whom I had a deep connection, allowed me to be myself and recognized some of the hurt and pain I held inside. She gave me the ability to reach in and deal with the pain. She also recognized my inherent love of bling and introduced me to the joys of turning those pages in the cooking magazine and of high-heeled shoes. I miss both of my moms very much.

But missing Tucker feels different. Sometimes it feels like it was a thousand years ago that he graced my life. Sometimes it feels like yesterday. There is an emptiness that does not seem to be changing. I miss the Boykin-ness. If you own a Boykin Spaniel, you know what I mean, but in case you have not had the pleasure, allow me to introduce the Boykin-ness. It's the constant ball in the mouth, it's the wagging nub, it's the tilt of the head, it's those yellow pleading eyes, it's the never-ending readiness to jump into anything wet. It's the love.

My feet dangle off the chair when I sit at my desk. Tucker always lay down under the desk when I was working, and my feet were always on top of his back. Warm and cozy in that pastel soft fur. Now I have to wear a pair of socks to soften the hard floor. And I ask why?

Yesterday was Sunday. It was cold, dark, and raining. David was pretty happy just sitting back, munching on pistachio nuts and watching football. He loves watching the game, and the fact that the weather was bad made it even better because there was nothing else pulling on him. I, on the other hand, don't watch football. I know it might be un-American, but I get no pleasure out of watching grown men bang into each other, get hurt, and bump heads and bellies. What is that? And do not get me started on what they get paid. I try to watch and ask ridiculous questions but always end up leaving the room. I did. I went to sit in my recliner chair to read and covered my legs with a blanket. And I ask *why*? Why isn't Tucker there? I did not need to cover my legs with a blanket when Tucker was alive. He would always follow me out of the room and jump up on me, covering my legs with his soft, pastel-brown furry fur.

We are approaching winter. Actually, we are in winter. It will be the first winter without Tucker. The first fall without him pouncing and running in the leaves has come and gone. The leaves were piled up and beautiful as only New England fall leaves can be. They still smelled damp and musty. They still stuck to the bottoms of my shoes and ended up on the floor. I just wasn't graced with the privilege of pulling the wet leaves off your fur and watching you disappear into piles of leaves. And I ask *why*? Walking in the leaves isn't the same, Tucky. Watching with great joy as you stuck your schnozzle into a pile of leaves, not knowing what was buried under there. Always wondering whether or not a mouse or a shrew or some other creature would dart out. And I ask *why*?

I was never ready for you to leave. You did not instruct me on how to do this without you. So, I ask *why*? I had no time to prepare for your departure. No time to internalize how I would live without you by my side. No time to figure out how this grief thing works.

Now, it is a Monday afternoon. I am babysitting my granddaughters. I am sitting in the kitchen with my second-grade granddaughter, doing math homework. Their fifteen-year-old Brussels Griffon, the first dog in our extended family, Buster, is nearing his end. His quality of life is poor. He doesn't really know where he is; he sleeps all day, he paces, he has a hard time getting up and lying down. It is a devastating decision they have to make. I feel every inch of the pain my daughter and son-in-law feel in trying to decide whether it's time and how hard it is to play God with a life. It aches.

Dear, dear Buster, how much joy you gave to the family. My second-grade granddaughter said, "Daddy said it is time for Buster to go see Tucker in doggie heaven. He said he did not want Buster to be in pain like Tucker was. It is your turn to roll the dice, Grammy. We have to find the even numbers."

From the mouths of babes come statements about death and dying juxtaposed against playing a second-grade math game. It is a mysterious world, this thing called life. And I ask, *why*? Why do things unfold as they do? There are no answers to many, or maybe all, of those whys. Life goes on.

My granddaughter will celebrate her eighth birthday and then her ninth and tenth. She will remember Buster and so will her younger sister, and they will both continue with their lives. Her mom and dad will grieve, and their grief, like mine over Tucker, will be a journey as individual as they are. The grief journey is not a stock item you purchase. It is a journey you embark on with no roadmap and no timeline. You know when it begins, but you do not know when it will end or where it will take you. Pack a big suitcase and follow that yellow brick road.

Tucker Bean, I miss you more than you know, but you probably do know since I tell you every day and write about you every week. Tucker, the leaves were particularly pretty in the back forty this fall. Tucker, in the famous words of Cecelia Ahern, "You will always be my favorite hello and hardest goodbye."

Bean, eighteen weeks in. I will love you forever.

    Mama

    I started the post by saying I had questions. When I taught writing, when we were learning how to engage readers, one of the techniques was starting the piece with a series of questions. The rationale behind that was that curiosity is a human trait. We seek answers to questions. Consequently, if the writing starts with questions, then the reader will be drawn to keep reading to find the answers. Some questions can be answered quickly. "Is there any milk in the refrigerator?" That is a question that can be answered very quickly and quite definitively. How about "Is it raining outside?" Another question that can be answered quickly and definitively.

    But other questions are not so easily answered. Why did cancer steal my dog? Why did cancer take my mother? Why did cancer rob me of a second mom? And then there are the existential questions: Why are we here? Are we alone? Is there life out there? What is our purpose? What is the meaning of life?

    I have no way of answering those questions. I am not sure what questions I can answer, but I can tell you the questions that I have.

    My birth mother, Julia, suffered from asthma and emphysema, and she coughed a lot. I remember them being akin to fits, but I think it is because I was young and afraid of seeing my mother out of control. That is so fraught with worry, and there is an inherent question that is posed with that worry. What does it mean for a child who has no control over her own world to see her mother–the adult–who needs to have control but doesn't possess it? When my mother would lapse into coughing spasms, she could not talk or catch her breath. Her face turned bright red, and if I tried to talk to her, she would wave her arms wildly in the air above her head as if to tell me, "Don't talk." I remember watching her gasp for air, and when she stopped coughing, I often felt it was my fault.

Question: Why did I feel that way?

When I was in seventh or eighth grade, I had a best friend named Heidi. Heidi and I did everything together. One summer, I went away to summer camp. When I got back from camp, Heidi did not want to be my friend anymore. She had befriended a girl named Jane. Suddenly, Heidi was now part of the popular girls, and I was kicked aside. No matter what I did, Heidi was done with me. I withdrew into despair and unhappiness.

Questions: Why? What had I done wrong? Why was I no longer her friend? What had I done to deserve this?

As a seventh grader, I was slow to develop, had curly hair in the days of straight hair, and because I had such a big nose, I was teased and called Tiny Tim. And if that wasn't bad enough, my younger sister was living the life I was unable to live. She was popular, invited to every party, and I was jealous. I sense, without having any evidence, that my mother was thrilled with her status and perhaps living through it vicariously.

Question: Did she like her better than she liked me?

Daily living at school was torture. I would often skip lunch because I had no one to sit with. The one time I tried to sit at the table where Heidi sat, I was told I couldn't sit there. They told me to leave. They told me all the seats were saved.

Questions: I was a nice girl, so why was I being shunned? Why was I so unpopular? Why?

I am not sure what precipitated the exchange I had with my mother when I came home from school on one particularly bad day. I would like to think it was a loving exchange that occurred when she witnessed my distress. I imagine a variety of scenarios.

"Sheila, what's wrong? Tell me. I can see how sad you are. What? What happened?" Or "Tell Mommy what is wrong. I can see it all over you. What is making you so unhappy?"

But none of this happened. What I do remember is crying uncontrollably, and nothing could make me feel better.

"Why do they hate me, Mommy? They hate me. And why? I never did anything to them, and they are so mean to me. So mean."

I am not sure if that is exactly what I said, but I know it was pretty close to that. What was I expecting to happen? I suppose that I wanted her to reach out and hug me, comfort me, tell me that everything was going to be okay, and whatever else I might have needed to hear. But something else happened instead. She was very angry at those girls. She cried and cried and began to cough. And even though I think that her crying was out of love for me, it tasted more like pity and helplessness. It is possible that she was crying for herself because she recognized that she was incapable of helping me. Perhaps she was recognizing her own inability to give me what I wanted and needed.

"I hate them for doing this to you. I hate them." I do not know what else she said, and I am not even sure she said, "I hate them," but I do know her crying scared me. She continued to cry, and I thought that perhaps she was crying because she was out of her league with a needy child like me. Who knows? But what I did know is that the crying and the heaving made her start coughing uncontrollably.

That is when the roles changed. Instead of her comforting me in my pain, I had to comfort her. It was now me embracing her. It was now me shushing her naked emotions. It was now me who had to take care of her.

And the questions: Was it my fault? Was it my fault that she was coughing? What kind of horrible person was I that made my mommy sick? If I was only this or if I was only that, would she like me? If I had been happy and popular, would she be proud of me? Would she like me? "Does she love me?"

Questions.

WEEK 19

December 22

5-2=3

I don't like not having my dog. It is as simple as that. Sometimes, I feel the void is so big that it is unfathomable to think that it will ever be filled. I walk down to get the mail. It is a one-minute walk from the door. When I got the mail and came back inside, Tucker would behave as if I had been away for centuries. Centuries. He would stand there wagging that nub. His look said, "Where have you been? I have been waiting." Now the only thing waiting for me is the garbage pail that receives the junk that is mailed every day. No wonder there is a paper shortage. Why do I need fifteen catalogs for curtains? I don't need curtains. I don't want curtains. I didn't ask for curtains. I never inquired about curtains. Maybe I should get some curtains.

A few weeks ago, I posted about doing my life without my LBD (little brown dog). I still do that, but sometimes it feels like I am just going through the motions. Do you get that? I feel tears well behind my lids as I try to decipher why the emptiness feels so cavernous? I have so many wonderful family members that I love, and they fill my heart. I remember as a kid, when I rejected finishing a meal and was told that I must not have any room for dessert, my comeback was, "I always have room for dessert." There was that one little space that was always open and vacant for dessert. That is what it is like. No matter how many other fantastic things fill my world, that one spot, the spot where my love for Tucker was, that one spot reserved for my Nubby-Bean is still empty, and nothing is filling it up.

I wrote last week about my daughter and son-in-law, whose beloved pet was nearing his end. I took it down off my home page out of respect for their own grief as they had to say goodbye to their Buster eighteen weeks to the day we had to bid our Tucker farewell. I hurt for them as I hurt for all of you who have loved and lost. That reminds me of the famous line by Alfred Tennyson, "'Tis better to have loved and lost than never to have loved at all."

That is true—I think. I certainly remember the wonderful pool-time antics, the countless hours throwing balls, and the first experience at a beach. Watching Tucker in the ocean made me so nervous I attached a very long rope to his collar. A dog bred for swimming; I was terrified he would get caught in a current and I would watch him disappear. But he seemed unmoved by the current. He loved being in the waves and chasing that ball. I couldn't wait to bring him back to that beach the following summer, but that never happened. What happened was cancer. So, instead of trips to the beach, we made trips to the hospital for chemo. So, kiss that kiss, hug that hug because you never know when the last time will be.

There are so many memories of Tucker. All of them are

dear, but the absence of the actual events cut like a serrated knife. I can certainly see the beauty of distraction when these bouts of sadness hit. I clean out cabinets, straighten linen closets, and cook, but in the end, when the last cookie tray is taken out of the oven and the cookie sheets are washed and put away, what am I left with? I am left with a tray of cookies that I am not going to eat. Not that I would have eaten them with Tucky at my side, but he was there gazing at me, hoping that whatever I was cooking would be for him. Those soulful Boykin eyes. You Boykin people know that look, those yellow eyes plaintive and hopeful. "Pleeeeeeease, I have?"

It is a strange feeling, that empty void, as I move through daily life. It's not that I would have taken Nubby grocery shopping; it's just that he would be there when I got back, waiting for the bone. The supermarket trip now feels pointless because I can't give him that marrow bone. The same empty void when I routinely travel to school. I get up, go downstairs, and engage in a morning routine. Coffee, paper organization, last-minute work. Difference: when I pick up the keys to leave, Tucker is not here to take that as his cue to run back upstairs and get back into bed with David. Now why is that such a heartache for me? It was such a little thing, something most people would not even pay attention to, but for me, it is titanic.

It is approaching Christmas week, and several of our children are going away to warmer climes. They are taking suitcases and their children, and we are watching their dogs. We would have had five to watch, but now we have three. Tucker is not here, and neither is Buster. I am so glad the other three are here, but it feels sadly different. Still lots of noise, still letting the dogs in and letting the dogs out one thousand times a day, but Tucky is not the first one at the door to bound downstairs, and he is not the first one back, waiting for me to slide open the door. So, like I said at the beginning of this post, I don't like not having my dog. It is as simple as that.

It is nineteen weeks, almost five months, and I am coming to believe that I will have to travel with my grief for the rest of my life. The grief will never leave. It is something I will always carry with me. Imagine, if you will, that grief is a suitcase with a broken zipper. My goal is to carry that suitcase so that the zipper opening and grief spilling out (like pairs of dirty socks falling out onto the street) will happen less and less often.

Nubby-Bean, just so that you know, I have written a book about you. It is with a publisher. You are going to live forever in the pages of a text that will hopefully help others who lose a very special fur baby. You, of course, are the star of the show. Tucker-Ridge. I will let you know about the release date. I miss you so much. Wag that nub, and please make sure you are taking care of our little Tootsie Roll, Buster. Please make sure he is getting used to it over the Rainbow Bridge.

And this is for you, Tucker and Buster:

It's Time

It is time to go to bed, my boy
You have played the day away
Surrender to slumber

To renew and refresh
When you wake in the morning
The world is awash with new things to learn
And off you go to grow
Knowing you will wake again to a brand-new day.

Breathe in the wonders that blossom each day
The world is fresh with newness and innocence
You reach out to touch and feel
The softness of the flower bed you run through as you chase that stick
The coolness of the stream that you jump in to chase that ball
The comforting scratch from the ones that love you
The treats they sneak you when no one is watching
The squirrel you can't quite catch
The tears they shed in your fur when they're sad
The kisses, the hugs, the countless "Who's the good boy?"

You can now surrender to the slumber
To renew and refresh
When you wake in the morning
The world is awash with new things to learn
And off you go to grow
Knowing you will wake again to a brand-new day.

You will take joy and you will give joy
Years of companionship and loyalty
Years of love and devotion
Years of comfort and family warmth

And nothing could be better.

And now the days are slower
Your movements more measured
You lie in the sun
Your tail still wags
Your head still gets scratched
The treats still come
The love's still there
The joy and devotion etched forever in their hearts.

It is time to go to bed, my boy
You played your life away
You can now surrender to the slumber
The world you knew must fade away
For your time has come to an end
You took joy, and you gave joy
You gave years of companionship and loyalty
They gave you years of love and devotion
You gave each other years of comfort and family
    warmth
And nothing could ever have been better.

Family love. The poem reminds me of the give-and-take in family dynamics. And I have to say that, in many ways, I am lucky. I have had many different families. There is the Mommy (Julia)-Daddy family unit filled with memories. Then there is the stepmother (Trudy)-Daddy family unit, which is also filled with memories. And now there is the Daddy-Meta (my dad's current long-term partner for over twenty-three years) family unit, which is still making memories. And nothing could be better because each and every union and relationship make me who I am.

I grew with all the grief that I endured. I learned from all. From my mother, Julia, I learned that it is important to be true to yourself, that being a rugged individual with a good heart and a go-be-damned attitude toward anyone who wants to get in your way is an admirable trait. I learned the best truth is your own truth because to try to live someone else's truth is cheating yourself.

Trudy taught me to believe in myself. Having confidence in yourself is the strongest weapon you have against others who will try to put you down. And it is the strongest weapon against yourself—yes, yourself. I learned that sometimes we are our own worst enemies, and having the confidence to face a fear or insecurity with honesty is the path to true understanding and satisfaction. And Meta, who, at ninety-nine, as of this writing, has taught me that women can do anything. A pharmacist and a mother of six children, she did it all before many other women even knew that being a pharmacist and an independent store owner was a possibility for women. They all persisted, and in many ways, they all dissented. Lessons that I hope I passed on to my daughters and lessons that I hope are being passed on to my granddaughters.

WEEK 20

December 27

Holidays are a mixed bag. Christmas day. Early. Gray. Cloudy. Quiet. Except for the three dogs we are watching juxtaposed against the dog parents who are waiting in line at Space Mountain or swimming in a water park. I have been perusing the various posts on Facebook with beautiful pictures of family celebrations, but the ones touching me the most acknowledge this will be the last Christmas with a pet or the first Christmas without a beloved pet. I have a sneaking suspicion, and I may be wrong about this, that many people who do celebrate Christmas may feel more lonely and isolated at this time of year if they are in mourning or worrying about their dog's impending demise or wondering when the grief will go away. I have a sneaking suspicion that many are feeling bad about feeling bad. They want to feel happy but just can't. I have a sneaking suspicion that many feel it is almost imperative to keep on a straight and exceedingly fake happy face because to do otherwise would put a damper on the Christmas joy and spirit. I have a sneaking suspicion that many can't wait for the day to be over so that they can just let their guard down and cry those tears that are pent up like bulls behind the gates of the pen. And I also suspect that many of you are turning it all on yourself. Why can't I be happy; why can't I shake this feeling; why can't I enjoy myself with eggnog like everyone else? Does anyone really like eggnog? Why? Why? Why?

The expectation of family happiness over the holiday season puts a great deal of pressure on humans. If you are not receiving a new car with a bow on top, if you are not at the ultimate Christmas party, drinking the ultimate cocktail out of the ultimate crystal glass with the most fashionable people in the most beautiful house where the problems of the world do not touch you, you feel like there is something wrong with you.

And, if you actually did receive that car with the bow, it is possible that you would actually give that car up in a split second if you could have your dog back or if you could reverse the lymphoma diagnosis. News flash: There is nothing wrong with you if you feel like a minor chord when everyone else is a major. There is nothing wrong with you if you simply feel that the colors, the glitz, the smiles, the laughs are falling on deaf ears and a deaf heart because you are simply numb. Because truth be told, you are grieving. Grief does not stop for Christmas or New Year's. In fact, it might even strengthen as you come to terms with what you had, what you wish you had, and what you actually have.

I do not celebrate Christmas, but I do understand the importance of family celebrations and holidays. I understand the dynamics of creating a loving environment that is filled with food and smiles and laughter and happy times. I also understand the bittersweet experience of being together with your family and taking joy in their presence while at the same time feeling disheartened and sad when you realize that your little or big friend, so much a part of your family and life, has been taken from you.

You think you hear her bark. You swear you saw him sitting in the corner. You are just so sure that he is going to turn up and be a part of that happy family gathering. But reality has a way of slapping you hard, and the hardest part is realizing that he or she is not going to come walking into the kitchen for a treat. Permanency is hard to accept. You go through the motions. You eat, although I bet you are hard-pressed to recount any taste. You smile, you listen to dinner table conversation—and then realize you are missing most of the conversation as you catch yourself thinking of other things because you simply cannot concentrate.

The questions flood your head. Why are they all smiling? Can they really be that happy? When did unwrapping presents become the root of all happiness? Why can't I get any real happiness out of unwrapping the paper? Does any of this hit home? I may not be opening up any presents today, but I am in the room with everyone who is and who is desperately trying to hold it together. I see you. I recognize the contrast between what you are feeling on the inside and how you might be looking, or trying to look, on the outside. So, as this holiday envelops you, I hope you find some peace in remembering your very special family member who is no longer sitting in the family room with you. I hope you can take some solace in the love you shared and still have. I hope you can feel at peace knowing that you gave your baby the best life you could have. Look up, close your eyes, and there he or she is. Standing on the Rainbow Bridge, looking down.

Christmastime puts you on a fast track to the new year and those resolutions. Do you know that research exists on those resolutions? Researchers suggest that only 9 percent of Americans who make resolutions complete them. In fact, research goes on to show that 23 percent of people quit their resolutions by the end of the first week, and 43 percent quit by the end of January. When I taught school, I always played a game with the students before they left for winter break. I asked them to take notes on what their family's resolutions were, and then we would graph them when they came back to school. The years proved this (not necessarily in this order):

1) Lose weight
2) Exercise more
3) Spend more time with family
4) Make my children happier
5) Read more
6) Get organized

Caveat: Because I was an English teacher, I think the "read more" resolution was listed because parents wanted to support the idea of reading and make me think it was a priority, but I can't really know for sure. But no one makes a New Year's resolution that welcomes pain and suffering. It is, for me, twenty weeks since I lost Tucker, and it is three days away from the New Year. I was not a fan of 2023. In hindsight, there were a lot of struggles and challenges. I am not sad at all about looking at it through the rearview mirror.

2024. I do not know what will come. I am sure there will be troubles, but I certainly think, or at least hope, that the positives will overshadow the negatives. Have you thought about what you will be doing? I will continue to work toward the following:

1) I am going to support canine lymphoma research. It is a terrible disease in pets because it is a terminal diagnosis. It creates angst and fear and so much sadness. And even when remission is possible, it sometimes feels like the proverbial carrot dangling on a stick because even if you can catch that carrot of remission, eventually, that carrot is going to be consumed and you will be left with the reality that lymphoma is a thief.

2) I am going to support the rescues because even though I could not rescue my Tucker from the cruelty of disease, I can help those who are suffering from other afflictions. I hope all those little Christmas puppies do not go the way of all the New Year's treadmill resolutions where the treadmills are tossed into the garage and the puppies tossed into the rescues.

3) I am not going to rush myself through grieving. I am functioning and functioning well. I have other concerns that take up my time. Aging parents, children who need me, and grandchildren who need me, but I am not going to pretend that I don't miss Tucker, my dog. He was with me all the time, and I miss him. I will continue to talk about him and reference him. I hope 2024 makes it easier for me to smile about him as my first response when I think about him as opposed to tearing up about him as my first response when I think about him.

4) And I will continue to write. I have found that it helps me, but more importantly, it seems to be helping others. I don't know how long I will feel the way I do. Some people may think that I don't want to heal, but nothing could be further from the truth. It is a burden to feel the way I do. It is not debilitating, but it is burdensome. I want to feel that I am on the way to moving on and fully accepting my loss, but I am just not there yet. Sorry not sorry. I will need to continue to find ways to smooth the rough edges like one of those really well-decorated cakes. The cakes where the icing is flat and even and there are no marks at all and they are just perfect.

My recovery is not smooth. It is still lumpy, like frosting that has cake crumbs in it. It is still uneven because the cakes still puff in the middle when being baked. I don't have a cake leveler, but even if I did, I do not think there is a grief leveler that would accomplish the same task.

And I have to think about what it means to love and lose. I loved him very much and I still do, but does that mean I should never love again? How can I never-love-again when it is so important to me? I have more than one child. I love them all. Is it possible to love another dog again the way I loved Nubby-Bean? Would I live in fear about all the things that could happen? What would happen if something happened to me? To David? Would I live the comparison game? Can I put myself through such pain again? I don't have the answer. I guess I have the new year to think about it.

Tucker, it is twenty weeks. Can you believe that? Summer is gone, fall is gone, winter is here. I hope it does not snow. I do not want to remember how much fun you had in the snow. Love you, Tucker-Ridge. You know that.

Mama

Just mentioning snow reminds me of how much I liked snow when I was younger. The older I get, the more I despise the snow and the cold. As a family, we skied. One of the things that I remember about our ski trips was the fun we had when we would go away with another family who had two children the same age as my sister and me. We would sit around a hot wood stove and our parents would go outside and do a snow dance–whooping it up and making funny dance moves. We laughed, and if somehow the snow fell overnight, we thought it was all because our fathers did a snow dance.

What I remember, though, as I think about my recollections and my feelings about my moms, is that I have a tremendous amount of respect and admiration for Julia. My mom was not a svelte woman. She was heavyset and did not move fluidly, BUT she tried. While my sister, father, and I traversed the slopes and weaved our way down the hills, my mom labored on the beginner slopes. She purchased herself a pair of tiny skis that were easier to maneuver. She said that having short skis would be easier to handle. She was short, so she wanted short skis. She wanted to be a part of the family activity, and no matter how difficult it was for her, she tried. She did not give up. She approached skiing the way she approached every other task she encountered, with gusto, determination, and an attitude that spoke to "I am going to do this." She tackled learning to ski. Snowmass in Colorado never saw a more enthusiastic learner. I am very proud of her, and I hope I have demonstrated that get-up-and-go in my life. Thank you, Mommy.

WEEK 21

January 4

What's the rush? Speed is important if you are injured and need to get to the hospital. A speedy ambulance could be the difference between life and death. The same can be said for slalom racers whose win or loss is often determined by a hundredth of a second. The faster the first responders get to the scene of the fire, the more likely it is that someone's life is going to be saved.

But in other areas of life, what's the rush?

Christmas and New Year's have barely left, yet the shelves are filled with Valentine's candy and plush hearts. We have not even had our first snow yet. It has now become a game for me to pay attention to when I see the first Christmas ad on television. I am generally busy thinking about early fall and apple picking when I see the ad. I am in the kitchen, the television on for background noise, and I hear the tingling of sleigh bells. It's September, for God's sake. So, why are there poinsettias for sale? And why are the Hershey kisses decorated with Christmas wrappers? What's the rush?

As if that is not enough, why is the Easter Bunny making

an appearance? Even people who are going to give up on their New Year's resolutions haven't given up yet.

School is out. The interminable month of March is gone. April, with its increasingly warm weather and its signal that the end of winter is coming, has passed. May slides by with Memorial Day signaling the start of summer, and the long-awaited June finally arrives. Alice Cooper coined it correctly: "School's out for summer. School's out forever." It is safe to say that by June 23, I did not have to wake up to gather my belongings and set off on my commute to school at 6:15 a.m. I could just relish the thought that summer was here and whatever I wanted to do did not have to be accomplished by six in the morning. I got up and went downstairs to have my first leisurely cup of coffee in nine months. I sit down, still in PJs, turn the TV on for background noise, and wait—what? What am I seeing? A back-to-school ad? For supplies? I am not even out for one full day, and it is back-to-school time. What's the rush?

Why are we rushing our lives away? We stand in front of the microwave, tapping our toes because, oh my God, it is taking too long for the microwavable macaroni and cheese to cook. How can I possibly wait three whole minutes? The advancements in technology have made everything faster and perhaps even more efficient, but they have also increased people's impatience. We live in a culture of impatience. We want speed, and we want things to happen more quickly, and we get impatient and frustrated when they don't.

Here is when speed does not count, even if you wish it did. Grief. Grief is pretty damn fickle. It does what it wants. It pays no heed to your needs or desires. It strikes mercilessly when it wants. It has no timeline. No matter how much you would like to put your grief in the microwave and have it over in three minutes, it won't happen. I think it is true that the level of your grief is commensurate with the level of love you felt.

I don't want to rush my grief. I don't want to wallow in it, either. I want to live with it and learn from it. Today, I heard from a colleague whom I'd always liked and respected when we worked together. She let me know her beloved pet had just been diagnosed with canine lymphoma, and my heart broke again. For her, and for me. I called her immediately and shared part of my experience. I did not sugarcoat anything because, with lymphoma, you can't. Lymphoma is terminal. Even if you get lucky with remission, the inevitable is still the sadness of loss. I told her that part of the struggle is managing your own pain and fear so that you can give all your best to your dog. I told her the decision about treatment is affected by many variables. Is it T-cell, B-cell, and what stage? Also about finances. It is expensive, and if you do not have pet insurance, it can be unaffordable. But no matter what decision is made, the right one is always going to be to prevent suffering. And there is no doubt that whatever decision is made, everyone who is suffering through this dreadful disease inevitably does what is best.

Grief. Today is twenty-one weeks since my Nubby-Bean left. I cried with this colleague. I felt all her fear, pain, anxiety, and sadness. My grief resurfaced with its crushing power and intense pain. But what I noticed was my ability to talk about my experience, about my Bean, about my loss, with something that I have not really been able to do before. I was able to discuss my experience with more acceptance.

He's gone, and he's not coming back, no matter what I wish for. Perhaps that acceptance is part of the healing. I miss my baby.

Nubby-Bean, you left me twenty-one weeks ago, on August 11, 2023, at 7:30 p.m. You took an enormous chunk of my heart with you. Sometimes I am not sure what this thing that is beating in my chest is. I hope 2024 makes it easier for me to smile about you as my first response when I think about you, as opposed to tearing up about you as my first response. And Tucker, to honor your happy self and your joy whenever you saw that blue racquetball, I will continue to try to help others who are suffering with the loss of their own Nubby-Beans. Say Happy New Year to Buster and Dexter and Buford and the Chelse for us up there on the bridge.

WEEK 22

I wanted to see Tucker and told David I wanted to dream about him. Someone listened. Here is the dream. I was in some sort of outdoor mall. Two sides of the mall were lined with nondescript shops. In the middle of the mall, separating the two sides, was a large area of grass. There were many people there. The ones I recall were people I have not seen in a long time. Many of them were teachers I worked with for years but have not seen since I retired. While I see them on Facebook, I don't see them daily, and the part of their lives that was a daily part of mine does not exist anymore. While not dead like Tucker, they are not here for me to interact with. I miss them. But there is a big difference: I can pick up the phone and make a plan to see them. You can do that on this side of the Rainbow Bridge.

On one side of the mall, there was a small shop whose door was open and was unmanned. My cousin walked into the shop and picked up a bat and a ball that was on the floor to go outside and play. And then I noticed a lot of those blue racquetballs Tucker loved to chase. They were rolling across the middle section of grass. I picked one up and called, "Come on, Tucker." He came rushing toward me when he saw me holding the ball. His face was smiling—well, you know, those looks that dogs have when we anthropomorphize them into smiling pups. He ran with the gait he used when David and I threw the ball that he tirelessly chased.

The world was his oyster. Have you ever thought about that expression? It means the world is there for you. Oysters make pearls, and perhaps your world will yield you that pearl. Tucker's whole world was a pearl when he could swim, chase balls, schnozzle us with kisses, and have Tucker-time daily.

I threw the ball, and he flew to get it. Not flying in the air, but with a great speed, as though he needed to make up for the time we lost together. And yes, the times we had together were wonderful and they are the fodder for great memories, but sometimes I fear the sharpness of those memories will blur and fade. I do not want them to fade. I want them to be crystal clear, like they were in the dream. As he raced past me to catch the ball, I noticed his fur waving in the breeze, looking soft and brown, just like I remember it. He got the ball and returned it. I threw it again, and again, he happily retrieved it. The people in the dream were watching us and began to warn me about the hill at the end of the grassy section because there was a dangerous highway at the bottom of it. I became wary of throwing the ball in that direction because if he missed it, which he never did, and the ball went down the hill, he would be in danger. I did not want to take the chance that he would be hurt and die. But something told me in the dream that I did not need to worry about that because that had already happened. The street posed no danger to a dog already across the bridge.

There was an apple on the ground that I picked up and

threw instead of the ball because my cousin, who was in the dream and who is a doctor, said apples are healthy. I threw the apple to keep him healthy, and he chased it. He picked it up and then dropped it from his mouth. He did not want it. It was as if he knew his body had no need for nourishment. He looked around and decided to pick up the blue ball that was next to the apple instead, and started trotting in my direction.

I woke up. I wanted to see him. I did. When I woke up, I swear I felt him brush against my leg. I did not want to let go of that dream. The rest of the day, I am sorry to say, was a bad one. It was a sure-fire example of the fluidity of grief and stages that have no borders. If I felt like I had taken two steps forward in my grief journey, I took a light year back. It was a busy day spent with children and grandchildren. We drove home in a harrowing snowstorm, and when we finally made it home safe and I was comfortably lying down, I started wondering why he was not curled up at my feet. The grief hit. The tears, the ones that burn behind your eyes, started. And I squinted to hold them back. It was late at night, and I did not have the strength to let the floodgates open. I am not sure why the grief hit me so hard and why I felt like I was going through each of the stages again. The anger, the shock, the denial. I sat up in bed and just looked out the window mindlessly, shaking my head and asking why. It was with an overwhelming sense of self-pity that I finally fell asleep. There are no words other than to say, "I miss your presence, Tucker—more on some days than on others, but there is no doubt that the hole and emptiness are still there. Twenty-two weeks sometimes feels like yesterday." This is what I wrote for you:

Not Ready

I wasn't ready for you to leave.
You gave me no warning.
I got hit in the face with a tidal wave.
A tsunami.
I had no life preserver.

I wasn't ready for you to leave.
You gave me no warning.
I was used to living with my whole heart.
I don't know how to live with a huge chunk of it gone.
There are so many things we haven't done yet.
Would you like to hear what they are?

Tucker, we didn't make it to the ocean.
We didn't make it to the sand dunes.
We didn't make it to the lake.
Your life preserver still sits unopened on the deck.
Next to the girls' swimsuits and floaties.

I wasn't ready for you to leave.
You gave me no warning.
I got hit in the face with a tidal wave.
A tsunami.
I had no life preserver.

I still question what I missed.
When did you stop sleeping on the bed with us?
Why did you stop sleeping in the bed with us?
Would I have caught something if I had been more
    aware?

Would it have mattered?
I go to the grocery store.
All those marrow bones I am not buying.
I avoid the meat aisle.

I go outside,
All those balls lying dormant in the grass
gathering moss because you are not here to catch them.
I sit in my chair. All those moments of stroking your fur as you rest your head on my lap—gone.

I wasn't ready for you to leave.
You gave me no warning.
I got hit in the face with a tidal wave.
A tsunami.
I have no life preserver.

Hope you are running in the snow, my snow dog.
Nubby-Bean, meet your brother, Cooper. I promise to love him like I did you, and I will certainly turn to you for advice. Kiss all the Rainbow Brigade members and say hi to Piper, Oreo, Bodhi, Cricket, and Phoebe.
Love you more,
Mama

A life preserver. They are designed to save lives. A safety measure. No one ever wants to use one, but everyone feels better knowing that they are available. A life preserver. They are designed to save lives from drowning. A safety measure. No one ever wants to use one, but everyone feels better knowing they are available. Harnesses preserve a physical body from falling to its death at construction sites. Narcan saves a physical body from overdosing. And when their lives are saved, people breathe a sigh of relief.

But what about what can't be seen? The emotional life. The unsettled feeling of loss. That part of your life may not be saved with a life preserver. Those struggles and pain are different. I write about not having a life preserver to help me with the drowning feeling of how painful it is to lose Tucker. The pain inside is real. But sometimes loss is different.

When I was in high school and trying, like all adolescents, to fit in, anything that marked you as different was a problem. Back in the late sixties, straight hair was important. So were bellbottom jeans, Danskins, and a whole host of other types of accessories that made up the uniform.

I had hair that did not obey that law, and my clothing was not part of the acceptable popular clothes that girls were wearing. In fact, there were quite a few things that separated me from the popular ones around me, and it created a good deal of angst for me. Often, I did not know what to do with those feelings. There was no life preserver to rescue me from feeling like a misfit and from how embarrassed I was by my mother, Julia.

I remember standing in front of the school, waiting to be picked up. It must have been in 1968. It was during the time when kids were allowed to smoke outside the building. The high school had a circular driveway in the front so cars could come in one end and go out the other end. There was enough room for cars to park. I do not know why I was being picked up or why my mother had to come into the building, but when she pulled up, parked, and exited, I became aware of just how out of place she was.

But it wasn't my mother who felt out of place—it was me. I would often like to have her back for an adult chat to ask her how she felt, how important or unimportant conformity was to her. I would ask her if she knew the level of suffering I felt, if she felt the same way I did living in the Five Towns. I would like to have asked her if she was uncomfortable but sacrificed her discomfort for bettering her children's education. I would like to have my Nubby-Bean back, not to ask him questions—that would be ridiculous—but to be with him so I could give him cookies and see those eyes again.

My mom drove a Rambler. I remember it being old and jalopy-like. It was far from the sleek, svelte Mercedes and Cadillacs that were more common. The car looked out of place, and so did she when she got out of the car. She was wearing her signature overalls and a hat. I do not remember if her coat was nondescript or if she was wearing her mink jacket. Tennis shoes were on her feet. She was makeup-less and walking with a purpose. I was standing among, not with, a group of girls who were watching her approach. "I wonder whose mother THAT IS," one of the girls said. "Weird."

I was flooded with emotion cascading all over me and through me. Anger? Humiliation? Shame? Pride? Love?

As I remember this, now more than fifty years later, what the emotions were and are, I realize that my current self would have felt and reacted differently than my young adolescent self.

My today's self celebrates her. How wonderful to stand tall, proud, and confident in an environment that placed stereotypical constraints on how women should act and look. It is certain that my mother did not need any life preserver because she did not feel as though she was drowning in a sea of self-doubt. But at that moment when I was standing among, not with, that group of girls, I did not feel pride or love. I felt the more negative feelings. And even now, I am having difficulty writing about those feelings because I am angry at myself and guilty at having felt ashamed and humiliated when watching her. I run the alternative conversations through my head.

"That's my mom. You have a problem with that?" Or "Didn't anyone ever teach you to keep your mouth shut if you don't have anything nice to say? It isn't like you are so perfect."

And all the while, I would be up in that girl's face, grim-eyed with crystal-sharp pronunciation and a "don't mess with me, bitch" attitude. But that isn't what I said. I believe I responded with, "My mom," not looking anyone in the face and dashing out of the door, feeling red under the collar. I have no recollection if I or we came into the school or whether my mom went in or if no one went in. I have no idea if I was angry at her for being "her" or angry at myself for feeling embarrassed or angry at myself for being so petty. It was so petty, my adult voice tells me, and my adult heart kicks me for feeling otherwise.

But at thirteen or fourteen years old, during the years when the party invitations were not coming, when I pretended to be on the phone with someone when I wasn't, when I pretended to be too involved in a book reading the same page over and over so the pain would not seep out, I did not feel it was petty at all. My pain was cavernous and huge and the only thing that mattered.

I read an article recently that described how the meteor that struck Earth, causing the dinosaurs to die, was a global event. The impact of the meteor set off a chain of events. It affected every continent and every living thing on the ground, in the air, and under the water. Everything. I had not realized the magnitude of that meteor strike. Colossal. That's what it was like having to deal with feelings that I did not want to have, but had nonetheless. Where was my life preserver, the one that would rescue me from feeling so devastated and angry at myself for not feeling like you-are-the-greatest-mom in the world feelings?

The love I now have for what was my mother's quirkiness and creativity was not discernible in those high school days. Age and wisdom have made me appreciate how special it is to not conform, and I wonder if I spent too much time trying to be the circle that had to fit into the square peg.

What could I have done with all that energy I spent trying to conform or feeling sorry for myself? I am not a physicist, and I do not know a great deal about the conservation of energy. However, a liberal arts education informed me that energy in a system remains the same. It can't increase or decrease unless acted upon by an outside force. While the energy stays the same, its form changes. I wonder how many projects or other roads I might have thought about or taken if my energy hadn't been focused on conforming. Conforming in appearance.

My mother had an energy about her that was often displayed in many behaviors that were both exhilarating and fun, but also rather impulsive and daring. She was a determined woman and went after what she believed was right and fought against what she felt was unjust and wrong.

When we were living in Far Rockaway, we did not live far away from the beach and often went there. I remember her involvement in making sand sculptures with us. We would dig big holes and shapes in the sand. She would mix up bags of plaster of paris, and we would fill the shapes. When they dried, we would dig them up and wash them in the ocean. It was thrilling to see what we had made. We would bring them home proudly. What a wonderful memory.

I knew no other people who would create such wonders at the beach. It was as though a typical pail and shovel activity was not even a consideration, and I am so glad about that.

She was a Girl Scout leader with one of her best friends, whose whole family became friends of ours. We skied together, did snow dances on the slopes to get the snow to fall, and overall, had a great time. Girl Scout activities were important, and we were all made to feel that what we were doing was important and valued. Our Halloween costumes were as creative as the limitless boundaries of her mind. There were never plastic masks or cheap, polyester costumes. The costumes were made with love, by hand, and were fantastic. Scarecrows made with real straw, ears of real corn, stuffed crows, pitchforks, and bales of hay. Cowgirls, complete with chaps, holsters, cap guns, boots, and fringed vests. And cowboy hats. Gypsy dresses with scarves and strings of colored glass beads. There was joy in preparing those costumes, joy in wearing them, and great joy in the pride I felt when I said, "Thanks. My mom made it." I did not need a life preserver for my pride.

There is, as you might be able to ascertain, a yin and yang dynamic at work here. Appreciation for her creativity, which I believe I inherited from her, and shame because I was embarrassed that she did not fit into my image of what she should have been, or rather, what I wanted her to be. Not an easy struggle, and it was a struggle we were never able to discuss and work through because she passed away way early. She died when I was way too young to lose a mother, at a time when a young adolescent girl needs her mother. Without the life preserver, I had to manage the conflicting feelings and issues I had, just like I have to manage the feelings of loss that I have over Tucker's death and its impact on me.

WEEK 23

In the summer of 2022, we planted a deck garden of vegetables and flowers in beautiful, colorful pots. Our backyard backs onto a large open field filled with deer, grasses, and coyotes that we hear more than we see. We are fenced in, so Tucker was always safe. He did not like the eerie coyote howl and met that howl with a low, guttural growl. If he was standing up when he heard the noise, his nub immediately went down between his hind legs.

Sitting on the deck in the sunlight or sunset, watching Tucker run around exploring his back forty, was a true delight. In the late fall of 2022, we began clearing the deck for the winter by putting many of the ceramic pots away. The furniture was secured, and the deck said goodnight to summer. Except for one plant. While all the others had withered and bade us farewell, one did not. One plant still stood tall and happy in the waning sunlight. It was not ready to succumb. And who was I to make that decision? There was no way I was going to rip that plant up from its roots and throw it away. It wasn't ready, and I wasn't going to play God. So, I took the whole plant inside. As I look back now, it almost seems like an omen. The last fight, the drive to stay alive, the inability to make the decision to end that plant's life. An omen of what I would have to do with Tucker in the not-so-distant future.

I never really paid attention to the flow of sunlight in the house, but now I did. I found one room with one window that got a little bit of sun. I moved the plant upstairs into that one little corner. As the late fall moved into winter, the plant shrunk from a large blossoming bloom to a tiny, fragile, one-stem, skinny plant. It had a few tiny green leaves. I noticed the one tiny stem had turned itself toward the window, seeking out the life-giving sun. I could not let that plant die.

Yes, an omen. This was a foreshadow of what was to come. Tucker was not sick in the summer, fall, or winter of 2022, so the idea of his demise never entered my mind. Why would it? I never even considered that I would have to live without Tucker.

I took care of that tiny, little plant. I made sure to rotate the pot. I watered it gently so that it did not get flooded. I put some crushed eggshells and coffee grounds into the soil. I nurtured it. It was going to survive the cold New England winter, and if it died, it wasn't going to be my fault.

Enter Spring 2023. It started to get warm. I started to get antsy to set up the deck because I am not a fan of winter. I brought out the plant stands and the pots, but it was too early. So, I came back inside to tend the plant indoors for a little while longer. And when it got a little warmer, I went outside and put the pot in the warming sun. The flower grew bigger and stronger and more beautiful than it had been in its first summer. I was shocked. Why was this plant thriving? It should have died. Why was this plant alive? Why did I feel so victorious? I cheated the

Grim Reaper. I won. I cheated death. I started to call the plant The Reaper Plant. It was sort of funny—until it wasn't.

In June 2023, I noticed some things about Tucker that did not seem right. My senses were aroused. He was a little more lethargic than usual. I walked into the room where he was lying down, but he did not get up. OK. I didn't think much about it. He turned down food. He was a picky eater, so maybe that wasn't so unusual. He didn't pick up his ball and bring it to the door for David. That was it. Not picking up the ball to go outside in the morning with David. No. I walked over to Tucker and bent down, and that's when I saw his eyes. His typical yellow Boykin eyes were bright red. Now, I was certain something was wrong.

I brought Tucker to the vet and left him there. He had a fever. She took an X-ray. He had an enlarged spleen. I panicked. She said it could be just a tick-borne illness. I was relieved. I live in the woods. He runs outside. It was going to be just fine. She sent us for an ultrasound—just in case. It wasn't fine. It wasn't tick-borne. It was cancer, terminal, and my world fell apart.

As I watched The Reaper Plant thrive, I transferred the desire to save that plant into saving Tucker. At the start, I was hopeful because there were many encouraging reports about remission lengths. If Tucker responded well to the treatment, perhaps a long-standing remission would be possible. After all, just because his form of lymphoma was a rare mutation didn't mean it was an immediate death sentence. Maybe his rare mutation would be the one that responded better to chemo than any other type of lymphoma. That would be just fine.

It wasn't fine.

In fact, each treatment proved less successful than the prior one. And as his body weakened, The Reaper Plant grew and flourished.

> I fertilized and nurtured the plant. It grew stronger.
> I cooked a fresh anti-cancer diet for Tucker. He weakened.
> I made sure the plant had water so it wouldn't die.
> I made sure Tucker had his medicine in the hope he wouldn't die.
> I made sure the plant had the right amount of sunshine to thrive and flourish.
> I made sure Tucker had a comfortable place to rest and sleep as his breathing worsened.
>
> I didn't talk to the plant.
> I talked to Tucker—all the time.
> I didn't kiss or hug the plant.
> I smothered Tucker with both.
>
> And now it is January.
> Keeping The Reaper Plant alive again is key.
> The plant still lives under my care and nurturing. It turns itself toward the morning sun.
> I turn the soil. I check it daily.
> The plant still lives in this earthly realm.
> Tucker does not.
> The plant should not be alive.
> Tucker should be.
> Nubby-Bean.

Twenty-three weeks and I miss you, still, like crazy. How are Buster, and Dex, and Bufe, and the Chelse? Tell them we talk about them all every single day. You, too. You live forever in my heart.

Lymphoma. Cancer. Mutation. Transitional cells. Protocols. Chemotherapy. Doctors. Vets. X-rays. Ultrasounds. Pain. Palliative. Enlarged Spleen. Blood count. White Blood Cells. Anemia. GI bleed. Side effects. Waiting rooms. Bargaining. Denial. Insurance. Deductibles. Nausea. Hospice. Death. Grief. Mourning. Grief. Grief. Grief. Acceptance.

Can you tell which of the above-listed vocabulary words belong in Column A or Column B? Column A–Human. Column B–Canine. Don't fret if you can't because you can't. None of those words are particular to the species, but all of them contribute to the pain and worry people feel for all species that are sick and dealing with disease.

If threes a charm, then I have won the unlucky award of being surprised three times with the news of impending illness and death. And each time, I reacted the same way. It's unfair, it's shocking, it's unbelievable, and it is not really happening. Except it is.

I was completely shocked when I heard Tucker's diagnosis. I was pretty certain that his symptoms were indicative of another ailment, particularly a tick-borne illness. But it wasn't. Being blindsided isn't something that is new to me. Trudy and my father were deliriously happy as a couple. Trudy and I had managed to calm the storms raging inside me that related to losing a mother whom I did not really know and accepting a new mother figure into my life. We had worked through a great deal of strife. I had grown to love her in a way that I had not loved my mother, Julia. She and my father were planning a big trip to celebrate a bevy of upcoming occasions. Their anniversary, her sixtieth birthday that she never celebrated, and their love for each other. Shortly before their planned departure, Trudy wasn't feeling so wonderful. And rather than going to a doctor in Haiti where they were going, she chose to see a physician in New York City.

Well, instead of checking into their favorite hotel in Haiti, they checked into Columbia Presbyterian. Her slight backache and low-grade fever suddenly presented itself as transitional cell carcinoma.

Surprise, surprise. Your mom has cancer. Surprise, surprise, your second mom has cancer. Surprise, Surprise, your Tucker has cancer. Yup, blindsided three times.

My mom underwent radiation treatments.

Trudy underwent a series of chemo treatments that made her nauseous, tired, and numb. The side effects were disturbing but manageable.

Tucker underwent a series of chemo treatments that made him tired and affected his stomach.

Trudy's side effects were disturbing but manageable. She had IV treatments.

I don't know if my mom had IV treatments.

Tucker had IV treatments.

Trudy's scans post-treatment saw no new problems for a while.

My mother's found blood in her spinal cord.

Tucker's scans showed remission for one week.

Trudy continued her visits to the oncologist.

Tucker continued his visits to the oncologist.

My mother needed no more visits. She left us.

A follow-up visit for Trudy revealed enlarged lymph nodes, indicating metastasis.

A follow-up visit for Tucker revealed enlarged lymph nodes, indicating metastasis.

Trudy became part of a study that was using a new chemical protocol. It wasn't going to cure her, but the best-case scenario was that there was a 30 percent chance that she would experience remission.

Tucker failed the gold-star treatment for canine chemo, and there was an even lower than 30 percent chance he would experience remission.

Trudy's doctors continued to be disappointed by her worsening condition, yet doctors also remained optimistic that even though she was Stage 4, it did not appear that a major organ was affected. The removal of lymph nodes was suggested.

Tucker was Stage 5, and there the removal of lymph nodes was not suggested. The cancer was all over.

Finally, a doctor, an honest doctor, told my mom and dad to do whatever things they had always wanted to do, to enjoy the time they had, and that there was no time like the present.

They went away, they drank wine, they ate delicious food. Those were their "whatever things they wanted to do." She was terminal.

Tucker swam, chased frogs, ate bones, and chased balls. Those were his "whatever things." He was terminal.

Tucker's last breath was on August 11, 2023, with David and me.

Trudy's last breath was on March 25, 1998, with a hospice nurse in the home where she and my dad lived.

WEEK 24

Last week's post took a great deal out of me. Likening the saving of the plant with my inability to save Tucker hit me deeply. In addition, the many comments I received related to a tradeoff between Tucker and The Reaper Plant also hit me. "Through The Reaper Plant, Tucker lives." I don't know who posted that, but thank you. It strengthened my reserve to save the plant.

What exactly is the topic for today? There are so many, but there are so few. I am unable to write about his last moments. That is still too raw. I am unable to write about the memorial that I have yet to create, for it cements permanency to an already permanent situation with a permanence I don't want. I am unable to write about the future thought of having another.

In short, writer's block. So this is what I tell my students who have writer's block. Write what you know, and just write how you feel. So here it is.

Just Without My Tucker

I stand in the kitchen
A pan of cookies in the oven
A plate of cookies on the cooling rack
Taste buds tingling

Sugar-sweet scent in the air
All of this just without my Tucker nuzzling my legs, wanting a cookie of his own.

I put the rubber duckies in the tub
The tear-free bubbles big and ready
The girls play mermaid and listen to "Rubber Duckie" by Ernie
They use their dissolvable bathtub rose petals
Their childhood innocence fills the room, along with the bath steam
All of this just without my Tucker dunking his schnozzle in the tub to drink the bathwater
While the girls giggle and say, "Tucker, no."

It is a gray, damp, chilling Sunday
It makes errands long and monotonous
Walking from the grocery store back to the car makes me shiver
The lines in the drugstore are long, and I am tired and damp
A bag slips out of my hands
Lands in the slush
It feels like an impossible task to pick it up and get inside
Finally, the coat is off
The chill is gone
I lie down on the couch
And sigh
All of this just without my Tucker jumping up on the couch and putting his head on my legs
Saying, "Mama, you're back. I wag my nub, yes? I

have a cookie?"

I look outside the window
The Reaper Plant window
It looks onto the covered pool
That is patiently waiting for winter to end and warm weather to come
The warm weather that will bring The Reaper Plant outdoors once again
The warm weather that will bring the flowers and the sunshine and the lazy days and balmy nights once again
All of this just without my Tucker holding the infamous blue racquetball
in his mouth at 7:30
in the morning
Waiting, waiting, and imploring
"Mama, just bring the coffee outside. Come on, it's time. I need to get in the water."

Write what you feel.
I miss you, my boy.
I miss your wagging nub.
I miss your schnozzle.
I miss you by the door when I come home.
I miss your presence.
I miss your love.
Life happens, just without you, my Tucker.

Tucker-Ridge, it's twenty-four weeks. It is too damn long without you.
Mama

WEEK 25

Grief is like the eighth layer of your skin. It is with you all the time, and it must be taken care of. Skin is the largest organ of the body, and most of the time, you are not even aware of it until its equilibrium is disturbed. You sit out in the sun too long. At first, the sun warms you and you luxuriate under its rays. Its warmth lulls you to sleep. When you wake up, you become aware of a pain spreading across your body. You are burned, it hurts, and the only thing that you can concentrate on is the pain.

Skincare is a $248-billion industry. We care for our skin because it protects us. We take pride in it. We cream it, wash it, moisten it, and it takes care of us, until it doesn't. Anyone with an autoimmune disease that negatively affects their skin can attest to how much they have to pay attention to all the triggers that will set off an inflammatory reaction that makes living with your skin less than pleasant.

Skin plays a role not only in your health but in the language. Have you ever felt so anxious that you fear "jumping out of your own skin"? How about feeling so insecure that you just cannot "get comfortable in your own skin"?

Grief is like skin. As you grow into your grief, it spreads through you. Like skin, the largest organ of your body, grief becomes your companion. It is as though grief has taken your good boy or good girl's place. It is always with you.

Tucker followed me everywhere. When I went into the shower, he waited outside the door, lying on the mat. He waited until I got out, and then he licked the water off my ankles and legs. I stopped trying to stop him. It was pointless. When I left the bathroom, he followed me.

If I sat down on the bed, he jumped up on it and simply waited there, wagging his nub, his eyes following my every move as I put away the laundry or folded the clothes.

If I went into the kitchen, he settled himself down on the floor, waiting for me to go closer to the treat drawer, imploring me with those beautiful, yellow Boykin eyes for a cookie. Me and my shadow.

My love for Tucker has become my grief, and I wear it like skin. Sometimes, it stings like a blistered sunburn. Sometimes, the grief is a little less virulent. Perhaps more like the pain of a stubbed toe. Walking, unaware of my feet's presence, until *Bang*. The pain takes a few seconds to travel from my lower appendages to my brain. And then *Ouch*. I am hopping around on one leg, and I just can't believe how much it hurts. It's just a toe. Slowly, the acute pain diminishes into a slow, steady throb.

Other times, the grief is more subtle. Like a pebble in your shoe or that sneeze that is lurking around just enough to make you uncomfortable and cause your eyes to itch but doesn't come to fruition. The tears welling in your eyes, the lump in your throat getting bigger like the goddamn tumor in his neck.

I wonder when it will end, but at the same time, I know it

will not end. It will not go away like that too-small pair of shoes I can give away. Grief is not as dispensable as we might like, and the hardest part is still grasping the permanency of the love-turned-grief.

Every morning when I wake up, it hits me again. Another day is here, but it is another day that Tucker-Ridge will not see. Sometimes, that is really hard to accept because I am used to things always having a beginning and an end. The day begins, the day ends. The school year starts and the school year ends. You open up a bag of pretzels, you finish the bag of pretzels. Beginning and end.

But grief is not following those rules. There was a heartbreaking beginning, but sadly, there is no discernible end. And that is not fair.

Nubby-Bean, it is twenty-five weeks. I miss you. We all miss you. Please take care of Buster, Chelse, Bufe, and Dex. Tell them we miss all their antics. I love you more!

MAMA

On March 25, 2024, it will be twenty-six years since I lost Trudy. I still grieve, but it is different. There are so many things that she has missed that she would have adored. She called my daughters the grandgirls, the fair young maidens. She loved them, and she missed watching them grow up. They called her Granny, and they loved her. She would have cherished watching their many accomplishments. Their graduations, their marriages, their children, their celebrations. But I think what I miss most is knowing that she would have been there for each of them to give them whatever they needed.

She had a keen intuition. She had an uncanny ability to talk to others and get others to talk to her. Point of fact. My Uncle Joe, now deceased, was a Holocaust survivor. He lost every single relative he had. He hid in the Polish woods inside a haystack, became a partisan fighter, and survived the war. He made a new life in the United States, but he had another family. He would not talk about his experience at all. Ever. To anyone. For decades and decades. Until Trudy. Trudy made him feel enough at ease to share his story.

She would have been a really good Granny for adolescent girls. She would have been a really good Granny for all of her fair young maidens as they became accomplished individuals forging their own career paths. She would have been a really good Granny for her fair young maidens as they followed their journey through marriage and children of their own.

But she is here in spirit. Trudy had a beautiful sense of fashion. When she was dying and knew she was dying, she made it clear she wanted us to wear red shoes to her funeral. We all wore red shoes. I still have the ones I wore.

On March 25, we still all wear red shoes.

WEEK 26

Six Months

Happy half-year angelversary.

You came to me last night in all your furry glory. I watched from afar as you ran like the wind across a field. While it seemed like the familiar field that borders our backyard, it was different. Larger, greener, accessible to you, not me. You paid no attention to me as you ran freely. You were happy. Your face was carefree. It wanted nothing more than what it had and what you were doing. I watched you being happy. Your gait was fluid, smooth, and rhythmic, like a wonderful wild horse running across the plains that don't exist anymore.

I was suddenly in one of the small bedrooms in the house. I was pretending to be busy folding clothes but was really on my knees, my head tucked down, crying, trying my best to stifle the sound. For some reason, I wanted or needed those tears to be private. And they were to everyone but you. You came to me and put that furry schnozzle on my shoulder. This is what you said to me in the dream:

"I am running wild and free. There is no painful breath. Please don't mourn my death."

I woke up crying and wrote this for you, Tucker-Ridge.

What You Told Me Last Night

You came to me last night in all your furry glory
Six months minus a day from your last breath
I watched you run, your gait so free
But you were not watching me
The sky was bright
The air was clear
In that moment and place
You had no fear
I watched you, Nubby-Bean
I watched you fly
It made me smile to see you free
Away from those things that bothered me
The sorrow and pain that I still have
Still sits with me each day
Sometimes it sleeps and lets me be
But other times it strangles me
You saw that when you came to me
And knew the pain I had
You tried to make me realize
Life's more than being sad.
"Mama, I watch you as your life goes on."
"I watch the kids grow big and strong."
"I watch you in your private times as you begin to tear."
"I ask you, Mama, what do you so deeply fear?"
I'm always with you, Mama, each time you think of me.
And when you do, I wag my nub.

And know that you can see.
So live the life that brings you joy.
And lose the misery.
Let your life blossom up around you.
I promise I will see.

Thank you, Tucker-Ridge, my Lemon-Head, my Nubby-Bean.

You gave me eight years of love and pleasure. It's been six months. I honor your memory daily. I look at your portrait every morning. I kiss your collar every day. And this morning, Dottie, who we are watching this week, came into the bathroom and licked my ankles when I exited the shower. She did it for you.

I miss you. Twenty-six weeks is too long.

WEEK 27

There are many things I have not had the courage to write about. His last day, the last conversation with the vet, the memorial I haven't created yet, the reason I can't open the Cuddle Clones stuffies that I couldn't wait to receive, but once I got them, I left them in their wrappings. There is just something about these topics I am shying away from. It's just not time.

Today, I got up at 3:30 in the morning. I knew there was no way I was going back to sleep, so I went downstairs. The snow was falling. There is something special about being alone in the dark morning, sunrise still hours away, and snow falling, illuminated only by the soft, dull porch light. And the silent sound. Things seem a lot more quiet in the snow. Did you know it is not your imagination?

Snow absorbs sound. The trapped air in the snow not only gives snow that smooth, silky texture, but it also absorbs sound. The sound waves get trapped in air pockets and can't bounce into your ears. So quiet is really quiet. And that quiet makes me feel even more introspective. If you listen carefully, you can hear the snow drop off the branches. The bird, the one lone bird that may still be on a branch, that bird's song rings sweeter juxtaposed against the still silence. It is a peaceful moment when I step outside, but also a melancholy one.

I like the stillness of the perfectly white blanket of snow undisturbed, except for perhaps the light impressions made by that one bird that should be south. Stillness in the early morning when all the winter creatures are still sleeping in their underground dens. It is peaceful.

I loved Tucker's excitement when I opened the door and he ran outside onto the deck and first discovered the snow. He would bury his schnozzle into the snow and sniff. He would then pop his head up, his schnozzle all covered in white. He would bite the snow and lick it, and plop down in it, and then get up and run down the stairs into the yard. I loved to see his footprints disturb the pristine snow. Oh, what a good time he was having.

And if it was a really good type of snow, the kind that binds together to make good snowballs and snowmen, it would stick to his fur in clumps and between the pads on his paws. When he came inside, he was very patient because he knew he would have to sit through the cleaning. From the large bone-shaped towel holder basket that I still have and can't throw out, we would pull out towels and dry him. We would use a wire whisk to pull the snow clumps out; we would use a hair dryer. He was not a fan, and all through the process, I would just hug him and call him my little snow dog. And then finally, when we were done, back to the door he would go, and yes, I would open it up and let him out because how could I not?

My little snow dog. And all the years we did that, I never once thought, "Enjoy this because it may be his last winter." Even during his last winter, I never thought that because I simply did not ever think he wouldn't be here. I never thought about his mortality.

Snow days brought out the slow cooker. Short ribs. He loved it when I made them. First, the short ribs get dipped in flour and browned on the stove. The sizzling of the fat in the oil and the smell of the ribs cooking brought him running into the kitchen. No matter what time of morning it was, and I do have a habit of cooking at five in the morning, he would be there, sitting at my feet, with THAT LOOK. "Mama, what is that delicious smell? Yes, I have? Me? Just a little? I have? Yes?"

And of course, I would slice a piece of the meat and toss it to him and he would catch it. And he would look at me like nothing could ever get better. And he was right. My little brown dog at my feet, sharing the morning and the food. Nothing could be better.

And when I made my first short ribs this week on the first snow day, I cut off a piece of the meat and tossed it, but instead of landing in his mouth, it landed on the floor. I closed my eyes. Tears inching their way to the corners of my eyes. Wow, wouldn't it be great if, when I opened them, I saw him licking the floor after the morsel was gone just to get the last little lick? But that wasn't what I saw. What I saw was a piece of meat on the floor, blurry because I was looking at the piece of meat through tears that had suddenly appeared as I was cooking, tears that suddenly appeared as they are now as I am writing. I picked up the meat and tossed it outside for some other creature to enjoy.

My little Tucker-Ridge, My Nubby-Bean, I missed you on this first snow day. I missed watching you run in the distance, playing in the snow in the winter wonderland you so enjoyed. I missed your rolling in the snow, your eating the snow, and how funny you looked with a schnozzle filled with snow. I miss holding you. I miss hugging you. I miss seeing you. My Nubby-Bean, how lucky I was to have you. How lucky I was to be your human. How lucky I was to be able to love you every day. Play in the snow up there, Tucky. And make sure that little Buster is safe and sound. Kiss Chelsea. Tell her she is a star in my book that is coming out. Kiss Dexter and Bufie.

Love you, Bean

Mama

I was lucky to have my Tucker. I have to say that at the time of this writing, I am still very lucky to have my father in my life. My father, who is soon to be one hundred years old, is still a very important person in my life. And he is a survivor. My father has experienced and beaten five different types of cancer. He has survived many, many losses. My two moms, his parents, siblings, and many friends. Yet he continues to live, and he continues to love.

An inspiration, I look to him for advice and comfort and realize how lucky I am to have him in my life.

My father has a special place in my heart and gave me many things that I needed as a child. In fact, in many ways, he was able to give me what my mom, Julia, could not. I remember my terrible fear of thunder when I was a child. It was debilitating. A fear so intense that I was afraid even on sunny days. My father tells stories about how I would be standing outside on a perfectly sunny day, but if the wind started blowing, even if it was on a perfectly sunny day, I would run around saying, "Koshe all the vintas." For those of you who don't know what that means, it means "close all the windows."

I was so terrified of thunderstorms that the only place I felt safe was lying in bed next to my dad, blankets and pillows over my head, fingers in my ears. And there I would stay until it was over. There was no one who could save me from the thunder monster. It left an indelible mark on me. Yes, I grew out of the fear, but even as an adult, I wrote about it. Here is something I crafted decades ago.

> What I remember most was the fear
> The fear of the black, never-ending night
> The clock that stood still
> No ticking
> No passage of time
> For that loud ticking I heard was not the clock
> But my heart pulsing
> What I remember most was the crashing, thunderous rumbles
> As the clouds met and battled
> Sounds so deafening neither fingers in my ears
> Head under blankets nor mountains of pillows
> Could quiet the echoes in my head
> What I remember most was the blinding light
> Flashing, illuminating, and startling
> A signal of the crash to come
> My paralyzing fear
> My helplessness
> My smallness
> What I remember most was my fear
> And then Daddy
> And everything would then be right

What a lucky person I am to have a father who is as loving and protective now as he was decades, decades, decades, and decades (I will stop now) ago. He remains a trustworthy man with whom I can share anything without the fear of being judged. My father is an honest and fair man and does not play favorites. Nor does he minimize his standards simply because you are related. If he is proud of you, he is proud because you earned it. If he is angry at you, he will tell you. If you hurt him, he will let you know. He is not a man to mince words, and he is a good listener. But most importantly, he is a man capable of great love and compassion. I am blessed, so far, with having him in my life for almost seventy years. I love you, Daddy.

WEEK 28

"Isms"

The suffix is defined as:
a) The act, practice, or process of doing something.
b) Behavior designated to a specified kind of person or thing.

Have you ever thought about the isms in your world? I have. Here are my Tuckerisms.

Tuckerisms

1) I miss your squeal. The one that emanated from your throat when we came home. It did not matter if we had been away for the day, two weeks, or for two minutes when I went down to pick up the mail. The squeal was there to greet me, and that nub just couldn't slow down. In fact, your nub is how you ended up being called "Nubby-Bean." And that is the name of the Tucker character in the book I am finishing. That squeal. One of the most endearing Tuckerisms.

2) I miss your schnozzle. Schnozzle, the name the girls created for your snout. You schnozzled your way into my heart.

You would lay that schnozzle across my neck in the morning the minute you sensed I was awake. That schnozzle and its soft fur tickled my nose and your Tucker doggie scent wafted up into my nose and I realized how lucky I was to have you, my Nubby-Bean, in my life. That Schnozzle. A Tuckerism that I will remember for the rest of my life.

3) I miss your imploring eyes. Those deep, penetrating eyes. Those yellow Boykin eyes. You had a certain look. It was very specific. It only came when I neared the treat closet. Those big yellow Boykin eyes melted my heart. The look was a look of complete trust and loyalty and total confidence that I would indulge you with a cookie, and you were right. I indulged you, and then I would get down on my knees and hug you around the neck and whisper sweet doggie nothings in your ear, saying what a good boy you were and how lucky I was to have you. My Nubby-Bean, my star.

4) That look. That unforgettable look. One of the most memorable Tuckerisms that stay with me and that I think about every day.

5) I miss your "talking." You would talk to us when we said, "Tucker, speak." When you were waiting for us to throw the ball, and we asked you to speak, you would give a muffled response—a little tiny woof—as though you were simply patronizing us. It was like, okay, okay, here is a little bark just to satisfy you, but we both really know you are going to throw it anyway because you like it as much as I do. Oh, how I miss that muffled woof. What a wonderful Tuckerism to remember.

6) I miss your private conversations with your bone. Most

dogs, when given a bone, immediately eat it. Not you. You sang to it. You courted it. You danced with it. I would toss the bone on the floor and you would nudge it with your schnozzle and prance around it, pushing it. And all the while, you would sing to it. Frequently, you would lie down in that Boykin sprawl and just stare at it. You would toss it back and forth between your paws until you finally decided that it was time to eat it. Then you would pick it up and move away. Oh, I can hear it in my head and remember laughing at you. "The Bone Song." It was, perhaps, the silliest of Tuckerisms, and I miss it dearly.

6) I miss your high fives. Remember how I taught you that? I would just absently lift your paw all the time and go "high five" and slap your paw. I wasn't purposely trying to teach you to high five. It was just a game. But one day, I just happened to say "high five" and up went your paw to slap my hand. Then it became a thing. It became a Tuckerism.

7) I miss your meditation hours, Nubby-Bean. You were an excellent self-soother. As long as you had a new Wubba toy, especially the rabbit, you could relax. You could smell the new Wubbas even before they came out of the package. You would stand on your hind legs, schnozzle my legs, and jump, all with that imploring look. "For me, Mama, yes? A baby, Mama, yes. I have? Please, I have." And I would give you the new Wubba, and off you would go, the Wubba in your mouth, the squeaker making noise. And up on the couch you would go and settle down with the Wubba and you would enter into a catatonic state. Your paws making biscuits on the fur of the Wubba—your favorite, the gray bunny—and your eyes would glaze over and your lids would

close. Your mediation bunny. My Nubby-Bean.

Addendum: As I review this writing, it is now 82 weeks since I lost my Tucker. I still write every week. I have a new dog, Cooper. He is also a Boykin. He is very different, but very lovable. That being said, in a recent shipment of toys from Wubba, one of them was the gray bunny. The one I lovingly refer to as the Meditation Bunny. I cannot open it and give it to Cooper. This was and is Tucker's baby. It now sits on his memorial shelf.

Namaste, Tucker-Ridge. I hope you have an endless supply of Wubba meditation bunnies. I hope you are happy.

I loved all of your little Tuckerisms. When cancer took you away, it made it impossible for me to be a witness anymore to those silly little joys.

I miss you so much. Say hi to Buster, Bufie, Dex, and, of course, the Chelse.

Twenty-eight weeks—like yesterday.

WEEK 29

Dear Nubby-Bean,

You came the other night. We were having a good time at the ocean. You were in your glory, chasing the balls through the currents, and I had the rope on you like that very first time we went to the shallow bay. I didn't want to take the rope off. You would catch the ball and I would pull you back, but everyone said if I took off the rope, it would give you more freedom to swim and get the ball. I balked, but because everything I did was to make sure you were happy, I took the long rope off. You didn't come back, and I woke up.

I am glad you came because I want to talk to you about something. There are days, Nubby-Bean, when my longing for you is so intense I freeze in my steps. There are days when I am far more accepting that you are gone, and I have to continue to live my life. It's like balancing weight on a scale. Some days, the grief is so great I am weighted down. On other days, it feels less painful and I function in a more carefree way, even approaching homeostasis.

The shifting feelings remind me of being on a seesaw. If you go down too fast, you are going to slam into the ground and hurt yourself. You need to let yourself down slowly. You have to balance.

Balance is important. Ask Dad or anyone else who has an acoustic neuroma. That kind of brain tumor can affect your balance, and when you notice that your balance is disrupted, it may be time to visit the neurologist.

You know when else balance is important? If you are a tightrope walker, you better be aware of balance, because if you aren't, your life and limbs are in peril. Acrobats use a pole that is weighted on both sides so the walker can balance themselves, which will allow them to resist falling and allow the walker to correct the position. I don't really know what that means, and I especially can't figure out how anyone can correct a position on a wire that is only one-half inch wide. That being said, the bottom line is that balance is crucial.

So here is what this all means. Nubby-Bean, I miss you like crazy, and I am clearly still grieving. I am learning that grief is a long-term companion, not a weekend guest. I miss having a dog, Nubby-Bean. How do I balance the life we had with the life I have now? Nubby-Bean, oh, how I miss many of your Boykin characteristics. How you would place that schnozzle across my neck the minute you knew I was awake. I miss feeling like the Pied Piper with you following me everywhere. To the shower, downstairs, to the closet, to the kitchen, to the couch, to the chair, to everywhere. My little shadow.

I miss your yellow eyes, the soulful expressions, the full and complete loving devotion and loyalty they offer. I miss their complete faith and trust. I miss giving my total love to a beautiful dog. It is too quiet when I enter the house. I miss the loving greetings more than anything. The "I am so glad you came back. I am so happy to see you." I miss watching the excited "pees" and the wagging nub that could propel a helicopter with its speed. And when the greeting calmed down, I miss settling on the couch with a furry brown beauty joining me, happy and content. Nubby-Bean, I miss that. And all those things weigh down the scale and push me toward offering my love to another, not a replacement, because you could never be replaced in my heart, but sharing my love with another may be a way to honor your memory.

Yet...

Balance scales have two sides. And there is some weight to add. I am afraid, frankly, to do this again. I can't imagine ever hearing the vet say, "Your dog has lymphoma again." I can't imagine ever having to live with the anticipatory grief as I did. I can't imagine ever having my heart ripped out again. Why would I want to put myself through that? I don't want to turn my kitchen into a pharmacy again and worry about GI bleeds and chemo. The worry of each day, wondering remission or no remission? I love you, I love you not. The gambling game. The lottery I am always going to lose. You have to be in it to win it. You never win it when you are in it.

And while I do remember so many wonderful things and have so many wonderful images in my mind, that last one, the one I have not really written about or the photo I have not shared, the one where you took your last breath in my arms and your still body let me know there would never be any more schnozzle kisses, rears its head at times. It is an image I push away, but it is an image that is there.

So you see, it is hard to balance. I am afraid to fall so deeply "in dog" again, but the desire to give the love I have and the knowledge that the love that will be returned is very strong. But it is juxtaposed against the grief that will come again. And the scales are not tipped, not yet.

Twenty-nine weeks, Tucker-Ridge.

We are coming into your season. Do you smell the pool getting ready to be opened? Do you smell the new bucket of blue racquetballs? Do you see me, Bean?

I see you. Kiss the Bufe, Dex, the Chelse, and our Tootsie Roll, Buster.

Mama

I want to talk about family. I have finally learned that the sadness of losing two mother figures has turned into gratitude. I am lucky because both of these women were so inspirational that I am who I am because of both of them. I think, and I can't be sure, but I think that as different as they were, they would have gotten along. I think there would have been a strong mutual respect for each other. I think there would have been open conversation and a combined interest in pushing to make my life as happy and productive as possible.

Mama Julia gave me strength and conviction, a penchant for working toward and achieving goals–but not necessarily needing to reach them. It is simply enough to try.

Mama Trudy gave me grace and confidence and the recognition that self-acceptance is key to fulfillment. Honest communication and being truthful to yourself are also key. And for someone like me, who hid many of my deepest feelings and fears for years, learning that it was okay to talk and let your feelings out without fear of being judged has served me incredibly well in my adult life. It is freeing to be self-confident. It is freeing to be yourself and give yourself permission to experience love, anger, grief, gratitude, and every other emotion that humans experience in this experiment called life. I love my family. I live my life daily, trying to make their lives as hopeful and loving as possible. I live my daily life feeling the claws of angst when I know I cannot solve all their problems and take away all their pain. If that could be, I would have it be, but like getting Tucker back, that is a wish bound to be unfulfilled.

WEEK 30

Dear Nubs,

It is one day shy of your thirtieth week angelversary, and I have been pretty busy this week thinking about several things. First, I have been thinking about the podcast I did with dogcancer.org, who reached out to me relating to my weekly writing about you, my Nubby-Bean. I have also been busy being pretty amazed at how many people I touched with that podcast and my writing. As of this morning, there were more than 3,800 reactions to what I wrote about you, Nubby, and your photos. And all of that got me thinking, because usually, by this time of the week, I already have a strong inkling about the story I want to share. So, while I had a few ideas that were milling around, it is what is happening this week that I want to share.

The expression "when one door closes, another one opens" is credited to Alexander Graham Bell. The next line that follows that expression is not as well known. It is: "But we so often look so long and so regretfully upon the closed door that we do not see the ones which open for us." Stop and think about that, especially the part about looking regretfully upon the closed door.

Why? I think people, once they are comfortable, want to

stay in that comfort zone. It is easier to just stick with what you know than risk trying something else by investigating the open door. So, what does all this mean? It means mourning over closed doors leads to missed opportunities.

You never know where you may end up if you don't walk through that door.

When my mom died, my dad walked through the open door and found love again, and I had a wonderful stepmother whom I adored. And when she died, my father mourned her death but was able to move forward. I taught middle school for twenty-six years. I liked it and was used to it but chose to leave and do something else. I got involved with another organization whose mission I believe in. I found I could easily transfer my skills to help other children in a different type of learning environment. I chose to open the closed door even if I did not know what was going to happen next.

When I started writing about you thirty weeks ago, I wrote because it helped me, Tucker-Ridge. It helped me process the deep shock, pain, and hurt I was feeling about losing you. I am not a naïve person, and I know mortality is something we all have to accept. I believe in trying to live your best life and do not like to see any life wasted. For those of you who follow the blog, The Reaper Plant is still doing well. I feel for anyone who experiences the loss of someone or something they love, especially when it seems too soon.

People grieve in their own ways. I have many mementos of you, Tucker. I have countless photos, statues that I paint to make them look like little brown dogs (but they are not as cute as you), cards, two Cuddle Clones that I still can't open (I know I have mentioned that before), your paw print, and your remains. Yet, with the exception of looking every day at your beautiful stand glass portrait that I had made, your collar, and the beautiful chalk portrait painting, I have not yet made your memorial. I know many people ease their grief by creating a memorial, but I can't yet. I will, in my own time, but I still can't. Perhaps, on some level, that memorial makes it totally permanent. The icing, so to speak, on the cake. The metaphor for me here is not opening the door to the feelings I will have when that last photo or paw print is placed on the memorial shelf.

But here is where a door has opened, and I thank ALL OF YOU. My writing is my grief relief. When I sit down to write, my feelings pour out. It is not planned. And I feel a sense of relief when I write.

What I did not expect, though, was how much my writing touched the hearts of others. I know good people can always be empathetic, but I was deeply grateful for the comfort, peace, and love that was sent to me. I was deeply grateful, as well, when so many people told me how I was helping them. And that was the open door. My goal shifted. Yes, I want to continue to ease my pain and work through my grief, but I want to do the same for all who have faced or are facing a grief journey. My open door has brought me to the world of writing for others now.

I found myself a publisher and am writing books about you, my Nubby-Bean, that I hope will help others. My first book just started off as pictures with captions, but a story evolved. I liked it, so I decided to find someone who might want to publish it. But then, I had another idea, and another, and another, and writing them was so cathartic for me. I started to believe that if they were cathartic and healing for me, maybe they would be for others. And many of my ideas are spreading into areas beyond grief. So, that is an open door.

I am continuing to write each week about my thinking in the hopes that it will help all of you, and I want to put those together in one place for people. I want to talk about grief and tell people how I feel, and I did that on a site that helps people face dog cancer. I hope my stories help you.

So the focus this week is not my Tucker and his passing. It is on people who grieve and who are at all stages of the grief cycle. It is a lonely road, even if there are thousands of us going through the same journey. It is a road that is scary and unknown. It is a road that no one wants to be on. It is clearly the road one would not want when Robert Frost writes about the "Road Not Taken." Do you know that poem?

The Road Not Taken
by Robert Frost, 1915

Two roads diverged in a yellow wood,
And sorry I could not travel both
And be one traveler, long I stood
And looked down one as far as I could
To where it bent in the undergrowth;

Then took the other, as just as fair,
And having perhaps the better claim,

Because it was grassy and wanted wear;
Though as for that the passing there
Had worn them really about the same,

And both that morning equally lay
In leaves no step had trodden black.
Oh, I kept the first for another day!
Yet knowing how way leads on to way,
I doubted if I should ever come back.

I shall be telling this with a sigh
Somewhere ages and ages hence:
Two roads diverged in a wood, and I—
I took the one less traveled by,
And that has made all the difference.

Like it or not, many of us are on it. And I want to help others the way you all helped me feel less lonely. I miss my boy; there is no doubt about that. But now, I want to take my loss and turn it into a road that will help. I need to pay it forward, so what can I do?

Nubby-Bean, it is thirty weeks. Thirty weeks. So long, but so short. I miss you all the time. Please make sure that Dexter and Bufe know they are characters in the Nubby-Bean books. Please watch over Buster and tell him that his little girls miss him and talk about him all the time. And, of course, give the Chelse a kiss.

Love,
Mama

WEEK 31

Wait, is that green on the weeping willow trees in the backyard? The swinging branches look like they have a slight green tint. The winds are gusting at forty-five miles per hour. It's cold outside. The week has been cold and gray. Wet. Dreary. But are those green buds I see?

Wait, is that a crocus? It looks like there is a little bump in the brown earth, but the ground is so hard. Is that a hint of purple? Trudy loved crocuses. I always knew spring was here if Trudy had a fresh crocus. She had a beautiful glass vase that held multiple single-stem flowers, and to me, it was the culmination of winter and the beginning of spring.

Do you know what a nanosecond is? "A nanosecond (ns) is a unit of time in the International System of Units (SI) equal to one billionth of a second, that is, 1/1,000,000,000 of a second, or ten to the ninth seconds." I don't know what that means, but I think it is fast—almost nonexistent. If a thought pops into your head in a nanosecond, it is a thought that goes away as soon as it comes in. You might not even realize you had it.

I had one. The pool company called, asking when we would like to open up the pool. My nanosecond thought: Yes! It's swimming season. Get that pool open because my Tucker-Ridge will be at the side of the pool with his blue racquetball the minute the cover is off. And in the same nanosecond, I said, "I don't know. We don't have to open it so early." And there were a lot of reasons. The weather can still be iffy, school is still open, and the kids won't be here; I am still working and won't be here. But the nanosecond truth is that the pool will seem empty without my Nubby-Bean anxiously awaiting that first jump in. THAT HURTS. Tucker-Ridge used the pool more than we did! So maybe we should save money and keep it closed?

I used to love to go sit in the very early morning with my coffee by the pool while the sun was still relatively low in the sky. The weather was comfortable, the sun made the water sparkle, and Tucker, my little seal-dog, would just jump in, measuring carefully where he should stand and jump to get that ball on the first try. That would bring me great joy. He could spend hours and hours in the water and often did. And last summer, his LAST summer, did not change his love for the water. I was the one who kept him out. I didn't want to tire him out. So I let him swim and then we left the pool. He rested in the sun. I think that he was getting tired, and he would not fight resting.

And when we would take our long walks, he lay down on the ground by the stump of Tucker's tree. I have written about his tree, but if you missed it, here is the CliffsNotes version. There was a tree about one and one-quarter miles from the house. The tree had a stump in front of it. The tree's trunk was really two or three thinner trunks that we bound together. He would mark all three. One day, I got a phone call while he was sniffing around. I sat on the stump to take the call. He immediately sat down. He was tired. His body was slowing down. So, that became Tucker's tree. I cry now as I think about it. My Nubby-Bean's tree. I think I am going to take a drive past the tree this weekend to see it.

I used to love watching Tucker when he spotted a frog in the water. The backyard has a pond, and frogs often find their way into the pool water. One of our children bought us a frog stepping stool that hangs in the pool and gives the frogs a safe way out. When Tucker noticed movement, he would jump into the pool in an attempt to get the frog. Tucker loved the water, but he did not dive. Do Boykins do that? Most of the time, he could not get the frog. He did, once, and he spit it out. Too slimy, I guess. What I used to love was watching his long-term memory work. The frog would get out or disappear overnight. Yet the next day, the first thing Tucker would do was to go over to the area where he remembered seeing the frog and start looking for it. I would laugh and say, "He's gone, Nubby-Bean. The frog isn't here. Go get your ball."

I used to love to watch him become my Tucker-of-the-Jungle. Tucker would swim and then rest and dry off in the sun, the blue racquetball in his mouth. But when Tucker got really warm, off to the planting he would go. He would bury himself in the plants, allowing the soil to cool him, with his head sticking out. My Tucker-of-the-Jungle. I liked seeing his head peek out.

Each first is difficult when one grieves. It is no different for human loss and canine loss because a family member is a family member. Just as anticipatory grief was the hardest for me when Tucker got sick, anticipatory grief greets me with each first. How will I feel when the pool water glistens and he is not here?

How will I feel when we sit outside relaxing on the deck and he is not here chewing on his bone while we sip our summer gin and tonics? How will I feel this first summer without you?

I Used to Love

All you did
You made me smile
You made me laugh
You made me appreciate the joy the world has to give
I used to love watching you eat up the simplicity of the life around you
A bone
A stick
A ball
A cool spot in the shade
A cold drink of water.

I used to love seeing you
And touching you
And hugging you
And kissing that little brown nose that perfectly matched your brown fur
So color-coordinated
I used to love that nub.

There was nothing fake about you
Your love was unconditional
Your looks so loyal and loving
And trusting

And complete
And it filled my heart with joy
I still love all you did
I still love your grasp of life's simple things
I still love the trust you placed in me
I will never betray that trust
I still love you, Nubby-Bean, with all my heart
31 weeks since you have been gone
That has not changed a thing
Well, maybe one thing
I love you more each day.

WEEK 32

Time flies. I hate using that overdone expression. It seems trite and canned, but there is a reason that phrases become so overused. It is because they are true. Time does fly.

Let's examine.

I am sixty-nine years old. Wait, WHAT? When did that happen? Eight p.m. is the new midnight. Four a.m. is the new ten a.m. Can't seem to sleep through the night anymore. My knees hurt a little. The idea of going out late is not quite as appealing as it used to be.

I went to a wedding last weekend, and we were at a table a little farther away from the music and the dance floor. All the young kids were on the dance floor. The music was too loud. We had to step out of the room for a bit. And wait, WHAT? All the people sitting at the table with us were, well, old. What was I doing at that table? Wait. What? I'm old.

Time flies.

My oldest daughter just turned forty. Wait, WHAT? When she was little, she wouldn't put her feet in the sand. When she got a splinter in her toe, she wouldn't let me look. She was afraid of Pippi Longstocking. She loved Big Bird. "Obsessed" is a better word. She used to tell a joke. Here it is: "Do you know green?"

That would make her laugh. She thought it was so funny. When her sister was born, she was two. After ten days, she said, "You can take the baby home now." She now has two children of her own. Wait, WHAT?

Time flies.

A prom. A date. A boy. Let's play the game Guess Who? No. Let's play Candy Land. I will take out the scary card. Let's have a coloring contest. Let's build a snowman. Let's bake little cupcakes. Let's carve a pumpkin. Wait. What? There is a boy at the door? You are wearing a long dress? You are coming home late?

Time flies.

I am waiting outside for the school bus to come. The bus pulls up. My father is visiting me. He is waiting outside with me. My daughter scrambles down the bus stairs and rushes into Grandad's arms. He is so happy to see her. She is so happy to see him. "Look what I made in school, Grandad. I made it for you."

I am waiting outside for the school bus to come. The bus pulls up. My granddaughters scramble down the bus stairs and rush into my arms. I am so happy to see them. They are so happy to see me. "I'll run to the house, Grammy, hold my backpack," says one. "Look what I made in school, Grammy, a fortune teller. Pick a number," says the other. Wait. What? I am the grandparent waiting at the bus stop.

Time Flies

We went on vacation. I laughed at you all in the bumper cars banging against each other at the amusement park. I watched you hand a bottle to the Frankenstein character outside the House of Horror in Lake George. You called him "Babastein." I watched you run and jump into the pools and dip your fries in ketchup. I watched you as you all fell asleep in the back of the car with your mouths stained blue from the ices you ate. It was only ten to one in the afternoon. I watched you all on the stage in ballet costumes or on the field with lacrosse sticks or in concert playing clarinet, flute, or violin. I applauded the loudest. I watched you proudly walk across various stages for various degrees. I cried at all three of my daughters' weddings. I wept tears of delight as you all went through labor and entered the club of motherhood. The most rewarding club and sometimes the hardest club to be in.

I watch and celebrate all of your happy times with you. I watch and ache for all of your struggles as you try to negotiate what it means to love so intensely and worry so deeply about children that you love more than you love yourself.

Time flies.

Time Flies

> You were a pup in my arms
> Squiggly, squirmy, brown ball of fuzz
> Tiny, warm, pink tongue licking my finger
> Big paws, little legs, long ears
> Puppy breath
> Starting life with your furever family
>
> Time flies
> You were a young dog

Bounding into the pool, retrieving anything we
    threw
Your favorite, the blue racquetball
You chased small plastic water bottles
Toyed with green plastic martini glasses
Your puppy-sized schnozzle buried inside the glass
Your tiny body sleeping on a big couch
Waiting on the ledge that looked out on the street
    for us to come home

Time flies
You were a good dog
Loved the family
Loved the kids
Loved us
You let the girls dress you up with crowns and
    bows in your topknot
You danced for them when we held a treat up in
    the air
They thought that was funny
"Dance, Tucker," they would say
You stuck your schnozzle in their bath water and
    drank it
"No, Tucker, you're eating bubbles. You will get a
    tummy ache. Grammy, Tucker."
Those were fun times
Time flies
Wait, what? Is that a white whisker on your mouth?
Are you resting a little bit more in the sun?
Are you sick?
Are you suffering?
Is the cancer taking you away?

Is the medicine helping?
Will my love save you?
Are you dying?
How did those eight years go by so quickly?
Why are you gone?

Time flies
It is thirty-two weeks, my Nubby-Bean.
Please, as always, say hello to Dex, Bufie, and our Tootsie Roll, Buster. Kiss the Chelse and remember that Mama thinks about you every day. Let me know if the colors of the Rainbow Bridge get brighter in the springtime.

Mama

WEEK 33

There are things I do not like. Dentists. I blame it on Dr. Dubrow. I would rather have a baby than go to the dentist. And just forget about root canals. When I sit in the dentist's chair, my blood pressure does something. I have to keep my hands either shoved into my pockets or put them together in a fist and squeeze them together. I do not know why. Long-term trauma memory. I don't look forward to dentist visits, although I know they will come and I will have to cope with it. And most of the time, when the visit is over, I am like, that wasn't so bad. Why did I make such a big deal about worrying about it?

But it isn't really dentists I want to write about. It is about memorials. I have both my mothers physically buried in cemeteries, but I rarely visit. However, I will say that on the occasions I do go, I get that same stomach achy feeling that I get when I park at the dentist. I can't really describe it, but it is the same. Once I leave, I am always glad that I went, and it is true that while I am there, while I am looking at the engraved stones with their names, I do reminisce and remember them, and when I leave, I have that same feeling that it wasn't so bad. Why did I make such a big deal about worrying about it? Even so, cemetery visits are not my "go-to" way to memorialize my loved ones who have departed.

So how do I memorialize? Whenever I cook a meal or look at a recipe or see a pair of beautiful shoes, I think of you, Trudy. When my children remember your lemon ices, I think of you. The first crocus of the year reminds me of you. You left us way too soon. But for me, the best way for me to memorialize you is to think about you. To bake, to recognize the beauty that you gave me while you were living. I did find a recipe for a triple chocolate cake that I think you would have loved. Moist cake, milk chocolate mousse filling, chocolate ganache frosting, with edible violets. It was you, and you would have served it on that Georg Jensen crystal cake stand.

Julia, my birth mom, I think of you anytime there is an issue in education that needs to be fought. Your feisty arguments with the New York City educational system left an indelible mark on me. Fight for what is right and just. All fights for liberties of any kind show me that you are still living. Finding a way to creatively help children ease their troubles and feel good is how I remember your attempts to make me feel safe. Stick figure stories, I still have them. I cherish them. When I write stories, it reminds me of what you gave me. Whenever I see a creative Halloween costume that speaks to crafting and creativity, you are alive. That is a way to memorialize you.

But what about you, my Nubby-Bean? Huh? The memorial to you has not yet been created. I have, as I mentioned, many things that remind me of you. I will be honest and say there must be some psychological construct at work pushing me to gather as many Boykinish things as I can. It is as though having these things will bring you back. I KNOW THAT IS NOT REASONABLE, but still surrounding myself with Boykin things must be a way to keep you alive.

I have talked before about what I have. Statues I paint, pictures, photos. I bought a Boykin-themed checkbook cover at the BSR (Boykin Spaniel Rescue) auction. I have your portrait and collar that I still kiss each morning, all these weeks later. I have your beautiful stained-glass portrait that Colleen Hendricks at the Glass Pansy crafted with love. Cuddle Clones sit in the living room. Your paw print in the Cornell bag. And any day now, I should be receiving the beautiful urn that Kim Orsini, a Boykin family member and saint, made for me so that you will have a beautiful final resting place. I have so many things that David says we might have to build another house to house it all.

But what does that mean? And how will I feel when the final "thing" arrives? Waiting for the urn makes it really permanent. Tucker's ashes still sit in the container from Cornell Hospital that has been, and still is, his temporary home. Not permanent. When something is temporary, you know something else is coming. Building a new house means you have to live in a temporary one. You don't spend all your time consumed with how to decorate it or what you should plant in the garden because you know at some point in the future, your permanent house is coming. Your permanent house will then allow you to move on from living in a house to creating a home. And then you can worry about fixing it up and living your life in your forever home.

Have a temp job? It is something to do until you have a permanent job that will allow you to pursue whatever your career goals are. Your permanent job will then allow you to move on from just working a job to building a career and putting yourself into a position to make a difference and do something that is meaningful so that when you look back years later, you will be proud of whatever contribution you made in your professional life. Permanency allows you to continue. It takes you out of limbo and puts you in a place where you can move on.

The limbo of constructing Tucker's memorial is coming to an end. There are no more things left. When the urn arrives, it will be time. I must practice the true meaning of Rest in Peace. I must let him do just that. I must take my Nubby-Bean out of his temporary home of the Cornell bag and place him gently in his final resting place. I am approaching that task like I approach my dentist's appointments. With a pit in my stomach, agitation, nervousness, and a little bit of dread. What am I afraid of? What if I don't feel the way I want to? What do I want? I am hoping to feel more at ease with myself when I close the top of his urn and know he is in his eternal home. I hope I do. I will not know until I do. I am hoping that I will feel the way I do when I leave the dentist—like, that wasn't so bad. Why did I make such a big deal about worrying about it? I will let you know.

Nubby-Bean, it is thirty-three weeks since I last saw you and held you. I hope Buster is doing well and is used to the Rainbow Bridge. Kiss all my fur babies. Love you more,

Mama.

WEEK 34

This post is a placeholder because there is more coming. Last week, I was waiting for the final Boykin "thing," the urn. I received it earlier this week but have not set up the memorial yet so I can't write about that for the weekly post. You already know I have trouble unpacking things that are related to my boy, but my goal is to do that this weekend. I will keep you posted.

If you follow the posts, I would like to update you on The Reaper Plant. If you do not know what I am referring to, here is the CliffsNotes version: I have a garden plant that did not die when all the other summer plants succumbed to the frost. I took the plant inside. It shrunk down to a tiny little stem in the winter sun, but it survived and flourished again. It is still alive, and I believe that it will flourish again this summer. I kept it alive, and it cheated death for a second winter (The Reaper Plant). Many people have said that Tucker lives through The Reaper Plant; maybe they are right. Is that a sign?

I wrote about a balance scale. Do you embrace the shared love between human and Boykin again, even though you know it is bound to bring heartbreak, or do you try to heal from the heartbreak and decide not to enter into that bond again? And many of you might know that part of my healing is writing. My first book is called *An Angel with Four Legs*. Tucker was my angel. Now, in comes a call from the breeder who blessed us with my beautiful Tucker. There is a dog, she is related to Tucker, she is going to have puppies, her name is—wait for it—Angel. Is that a sign?

I wrote about triggers. My favorite trigger was Roy Rogers's palomino horse. But I did not write about that trigger. I wrote about how, all of a sudden, almost everything you see or hear becomes a trigger that resurrects your loss. Can't go down the dog food aisle? Cooking for your dog? Can't go past the meat section? Was that your favorite street to walk on? Take an alternate route. Triggers can cripple you. We have children who have lots of dogs, past and present. A lot of our children's dogs are becoming characters in my books—either as canine or human characters. Jack, one of our children's dogs, is a great boy. He sings when you tell him to sing. He loves to lie in the sun. He loves to be outside. He loves to sleep on the pillow your head is on. He has mast cell carcinoma. Trigger. David took him to the vet. Our vet's office is decorated with photos of all their animal patients. Tucker's two pictures are still on the wall. Trigger. The vet said she wanted to consult with an oncologist. Double trigger. She prescribed prednisone. Triple trigger. What can I say? I picked up the prescription and got some pill poppers. Way back, way way back, at the very beginning of the writing, I wrote about a glass I had. A perfect scotch glass, it also became a perfect glass to hold Tucker's meds. I don't have it anymore. I just took Jack's meds out of the container from the pharmacy. I had to get rid of the glass, but the idea of prednisone for dogs: trigger. But we have to survive those triggers. Jack—I fear his future. I will let you know.

Time flies. I have written about time lots of times. How it waits for no one. How it either lags or flies. How it can be a friend—"time heals all wounds"—or an enemy, where each passing day reminds you that you have an endless number of days ahead of you without your lost baby. The truth is, time is a constant and it will have to pass and it is up to you how you are going to deal with each passing day. Time has not taken away my grief; I do not think it ever will, but it has softened the blow a little bit, sometimes, not all the time, but sometimes, and I have to be grateful for that. I will keep you posted on my memorial challenge.

Nubby-Bean. It has been thirty-four weeks. I hope I will find the strength to allow you to settle into your resting place, although I know your final resting place is in my heart, not in the beautiful urn. I hope you are spending time with the Chelse, our Tootsie Roll, Buster, Dex, and Bufie. The whole family misses each and every one of you guys. Oh, Nani and Lilah want to know: Are there any unicorns up there on the Rainbow Bridge?

Mama loves you.

WEEK 35

It was Saturday morning, April 6. I graded the papers, did the laundry, emptied the dishwasher, cleaned the refrigerator, and had coffee. David got up. We could have started the memorial. But it was early, and I didn't have to do it right away. I had the whole day.

Well, what am I waiting for? When I started writing about the Cuddle Clones, I talked about my fear. Fear I would fall apart if the stuffie did not look like Tucker, and my hopes about having him here with me would be dashed. Or I would fall apart because the likeness would be so uncanny that I would be stricken twice with loss. I mentioned last week that I had received the urn, and I was hoping to find the strength to create the final resting place memorial for my boy.

There are so many steps involved in the task. Finding a space, deciding what goes where, what things to include or not include, what should be opened first. So many decisions. I do not know what weekly post it was when I wrote about being an English teacher who has to teach nonfiction text structures, but I wrote about how grief could fit into one of those structures. I can see how all of them (problem-solution, descriptive, sequential timeline, compare and contrast, cause and effect) relate to grieving and making the memorial.

I had a problem. How to start creating the memorial. Here was the solution: Pick something and get started. So, I did. When David walked into the kitchen, I said, "It's time to open one of the Cuddle Clones."

We walked into the den and picked up the packages, the ones that had been sitting in the corner since October 2023. I picked up one and unwrapped it with my eyes closed. I ran my hands up and down the stuffie and knew from the touch that the Cuddle Clones company had gotten the texture of his fur absolutely correct. I felt around for the top of his head, and my heart skipped a beat or ten because I knew the topknot was spot-on. I felt the tongue: flat and long—yup. I felt the nub. It was a Boykin nub. I had to see it. It was time.

I bought two of them. I needed to have one that would be Tucker lying down and another with Tucker sitting up. When I opened my eyes, I could not believe what I saw. I can't believe how close the rendition was to my boy. It was hard to believe that someone could create a stuffed animal so accurately. I cried. It reminded me of how much I loved and still love my Nubby-Bean. It brought back the good memories of him sitting on my lap or lying on the floor or sitting in the chair or lying on the couch. It was a good cry.

I ordered the clones in September 2023. I received them in October 2023. I put them in my den, and there they sat for six months until I found the strength to open them. I am glad I did. I do not regret waiting because, with grief, you set your own pace. I waited six months because I wasn't ready before. I was ready that

Saturday.

His ashes—not so much. The following day was Sunday. I brought the Cuddle Clone to my dad. He is ninety-eight and a half years old. He really loved Tucker. He knew how much I loved Tucker. When he saw the stuffie, his breath caught in his mouth and tears came to his eyes. "Oh my God," he said. Enough said.

Have you ever climbed to the top of a high-diving board feeling like you were going to do it but then backed down because, damn, when you looked down from the top of the diving board, it was too far, and what if you belly-flopped down and got hurt? Nah, so you back down and figure you can try it some other day, or week, or maybe even next summer. But you are making progress because, at first, you would not even consider the high board. Then, you walked up a couple of steps, then you finally made it to the top and found the courage to walk out to the end before you backed down. Okay, progress.

Such is my tribute to Tucky. It has been progressing. The Cuddle Clones have been opened, and they have taken their place in our home. I love them. One is in Tucky's bed, and the other is upstairs. They remind me of my boy. They make me smile.

I came home from work on Thursday and saw the boxes that held the urns that Kim Orsini (love you, Kim) crafted. I climbed up a few steps of the high-diving board ladder. I brought the box into the kitchen. I climbed another step. I opened the box and took out two beautifully and carefully wrapped urns. I climbed another step. I gave one of the urns to David, and he opened it. My stomach was a little agitated, but it was just beautiful. The first urn that Kim made had slightly chipped during firing, so she crafted another. Another step. I opened the other box and unwrapped the urn that I knew was going to be Nubby-Bean's final resting place. I placed the two next to each other. I looked at them, and first, I marveled at how beautifully crafted they were. I made eye contact with David across the table. He was watching me. My next thoughts were, here it is, Tucker's final resting place. He can come out of the Cornell bag, out of his temporary home, and be placed in his permanent home within his home.

I took the two urns and placed them on the shelf next to Tucker's bag. I was on the top of the diving board ladder, but I decided I had to back down. I know the urns are where they need to be. I know my boy must be gently placed inside, but not today.

We left home to have dinner with one of our children. I packed up my Cuddle Clone in a shopping bag to bring it to the restaurant to show it to my daughter. When we were leaving the restaurant, a couple was walking in, and the woman gasped, "Oh my God, I thought it was real." I then told her about Tucker and the stuffies and how much I miss him. And she said, "Well, aren't you glad I thought it was real? Now it will be like he is really there with you."

And I replied, "Yes."

Nubby-Bean, the truth is you will always be with me. The physical resemblance of the Clones is a wonderful reminder, but you live in my heart. I promise to make sure that you will be placed peacefully in your home soon. Thirty-five weeks, my boy. You are missed. And as usual, please hug and kiss our Tootsie Roll, Buster, our Dex, Bufie, and the wonderful Chelse.

WEEK 36

Firsts are hard. The first time you have to step away as a parent when he or she takes that first step, and you know it is only moving forward from then on. The first time you get a "No, I can do it myself," you realize that your baby is on the move to becoming an independent human being with a mind of his or her own. A separate individual who will not need you in the same way anymore.

What about that first step onto the school bus, and now her day is being spent with others, and as you walk away from the bus stop, you realize that as soon as you get into the house, you're going to break down into tears because you are seeing the passage of time. The first time you have to pick her up from the mall because she wants to go with her friends instead of staying home and looking at old photo albums. What about the first driver's permit and the first time he drives away by himself and your stomach turns because now there is a worry that you never anticipated? The first date, staring at your watch and wondering whether or not they are—well, you know, and how relieved you are when the door opens and she is home. What about that first time they are late getting home and wait—what? There is a boyfriend or a girlfriend. The first gray hair. The first baby your baby has.

Firsts are hard. I do not know if they ever get better.

What about the first time you have to say goodbye to your fur baby? What about every first after that? I may have mentioned once or twice or ten thousand times that I was not ready for Tucker to go. I wasn't ready, but the biggest thing was I just never imagined that I would have to do this. So the whole idea of having to say goodbye was a first that I was unprepared for. Firsts are really hard, and when the realization of the first hits you, it knocks you over and brings you right back to the pain and disbelief. Why are you dead? Why did you leave? Why am I suffering so much?

I don't usually count the days in terms of my writing. That being said, it is Monday. Urns are here, but his remains are still in the bag. Maybe this week, maybe not. He loves me, he loves me not.

It is so warm today that when I looked outside the window, I suddenly realized this was going to be the first summer without Tucker waiting for the pool to open. I swear, I think he was able to smell the season change. I swear, I think he was always counting down in his head. Pool minus two weeks until opening. P minus one week until opening. P minus zero. Jump.

When I looked at the pool cover, it just hit so hard. I am going to open it, I will put the floats in, I will appreciate how pretty it looks, but damn it to hell and beyond—my little brown swimmer is not jumping in. The mornings had a specific routine. Early morning meant coffee by the pool. The warm coffee and the still, cool air of the morning. The sun was bright enough to make the droplets of water that Tucker shook off his body glisten, but not so hot that I was uncomfortable. The streets were still quiet, and frankly, the promise of a nice day was wrapped up for the taking. I cherished those mornings. Whether or not I choose to have coffee outside this summer is not known yet, but what is known is that if I do, it is going to be a difficult first.

There will be a few other firsts headed in my direction, and I suspect the next first will occur this weekend—the day after this post because I am going to try to rehome my Tucker into his permanent home. Wish me luck.

Thirty-six weeks, my Tucky boy. I miss you. We all do. You know the drill. Kiss Bufie and Dex. Tell them we miss them. Hey, Tootsie Roll Buster, hope you are having fun up there, and Chelse, you know we miss you.

Love you, Tucker-Ridge.

Mama

WEEK 37

My stomach is rumbling, and it is not because I had some hot salsa. It is because it is Thursday afternoon at 4 p.m. I am extremely dedicated to documenting my grief journal weekly. And here it is about twelve hours from when I generally post, and there is no memorial yet.

It is only twenty steps from where I am sitting to the blue Cornell Veterinary bag that holds my Nubby-Bean's remains in the other room. I am only twenty steps away from the urns that were made to hold Tucker's remains. I am only twenty steps away from the wrapped paw print Cornell made for me. It is in the bag with his remains. I am only twenty steps away from the sympathy card that I know expresses sorrow and condolences from the wonderful staff at the hospital. It still rests in the bag. I am only twenty steps away from the rainbow candle, the pictures, and the glass bowl containing his favorite blue racquetballs.

Twenty steps. That is not very far. Twenty steps. Do you know what the training ritual is for someone who wants to run a marathon? It is a carefully thought-out plan designed to build tolerance and resistance. You don't just wake up one morning, throw back some carbs, put on your Keds, and run twenty-six miles. You have to build your ability to maintain a steady speed, you have to slowly work up the strength in your legs so that your muscles don't plan a revolution against you. "Wait, we have been sitting around for years, and now you want us to do what?" Slow and steady. And there is more than building your physical strength. Your mental acuity needs sharpening and training. You must be the master of your mind. You have to focus on your task. You must train your brain to concentrate and think only about putting one foot in front of the other. You have to build your ability to push through the cramps, the stomach pangs, the dizziness that might strike you. In short, you have to be prepared to start the task and finish the task.

Finishing the marathon certainly brings a sense of relief. Months and months of training. Total focus on the preparation. It controlled how you lived. And now, it is over. Yes, you did it; you made it through. But be careful because it is more likely than not that your body might revolt with Delayed Onset Muscle Soreness, which might cripple you for a while. Or the Post-Race Blues might hit. What now? What will you do now? After all, your whole life was training for that race. And now that you have accomplished your goal, there might be a letdown of some sort.

Did you know there are 55,000 steps in a marathon, give or take a few? It takes a lot of work and time to prepare yourself to run 55,000 steps. You run a regimented number of steps each day, gradually increasing your mileage. Build strength. Build stamina. I only have twenty steps. It is my marathon.

I believe that my talking over the last few weeks about this memorial is like beginning to train for a marathon. It gives me the chance to process and think about its importance. I want to create something that will demonstrate my love for my boy. Trying to decide what things, all those items I have talked about, will be in the memorial is another step in my marathon training. All my mementos are dear to me, but I want to choose the most meaningful ones. And in doing so, I continue to process my sadness about my loss, but I am building memories about the joy he gave me. Step by step.

Grief has no timeline. It comes, and it stays. It never leaves. You learn to live with it and around it. I will get there. I will not force it. However, as in training for a marathon, you need to increase your mileage. The Cornell tin that holds his remains is out of the bag and on the shelf. And that is all I can do.

It's thirty-seven weeks, Nubby-Bean. The weather is getting nicer. The willow trees are getting green. The Tucker-of-the-Jungle plants are still in winter mode. The pool is still closed. I miss you every day. Two of the Nubby-Bean books are done. You are the star.

As always, kiss the Tootsie Roll, Buster. Hug Dex and Bufie. And make sure the Chelse is happy up there.

Love you more,

Mama

WEEK 38

In the many months I have been writing and reading many posts by others who are grieving, I can see there is a commonality. It is the oh-so-true adage that dogs will give you the best days of your lives and one of the worst days ever. You know the expression misery loves company? Well, it is true in the sense that it makes you feel less alone, less isolated. It isn't so much that you want others to be miserable with you; it's just that it gives you a sense of connection. A sense of empathy. An I-know-how-you-feel and I-wish-I-could-help-you sort of feeling.

I read a recent article in *The Atlantic* that tried to explain why we grieve so deeply when we lose our dogs. The author researched the connection between people and dogs because of his curiosity as to why he shed more tears for his dog than he did for one of his parents. It wasn't that he did not suffer the loss of his mother, but there was something so different when his dog died. This feeling is so prevalent that it has led to many memes; one of them states, "I don't care who dies in the movie as long as the dog lives." Do you have the T-shirt? I have been tempted to buy it often. If you research this phenomenon yourself, you can find dozens of people who feel they need to get some professional help because with every year that passes, they realize their dog is one year closer to his or her demise, and that is a thought many people can't live with. The connection between human and dog has existed for ten to fifteen thousand years—give or take a few millennia. So, why wouldn't we grieve the way we do?

Tucker's last day started off like they all do. It was summer. It was hot. There were blue balls to chase and dive after and that is what we did. It was a Friday. I was getting ready to go away the following day to a high school reunion—fifty years. In the afternoon, as we were sitting around, I noticed an increase in Tucker's panting. Prednisone causes that, but this was different. I told you that I believe I was so attuned to how he was feeling that I knew before he did when he needed to see a vet. It was early evening; the only vet that was open was the ER vet at Cornell, where he was receiving chemo treatments. He was not due for another treatment for a week, but I was going away and I just wanted to bring him in to have him stabilized to see if there was something that could ease his panting.

When we arrived at the vet and gave our name, the first thing they did was call "TRIAGE!" Triage sounded serious. I was only there for stabilization. Several people immediately came out to the waiting room and took my Nubby-Bean to the back room for evaluation. I was only there for stabilization. While he was there, I did what I always did. Pace. From one end of the waiting room to the other. Back and forth. Back and forth. I am not sure how much time passed. Was it ten minutes? Thirty? Ninety? I have no concept of time. One of the vets came out and told us they were trying to calm Tucker down. They had him in an oxygen crate with extra O2, but that did not seem to help him. I only came for stabilization. They suggested we wait a little longer. They gave him a sedative to calm him down. A sedative? Why? I just came to get him stabilized.

When they came back out, the news from the critical care vet who was working was very grim. The words were received through my ear. The words were processed in my brain. I could not comprehend the meaning of what he was saying: "…your dog's lungs are riddled with disease. We compared the X-ray that was taken two days ago to the X-ray we took in June when he was diagnosed, and the disease has progressed. It has metastasized into his lungs. He is having trouble breathing."

Metastatic disease? My Tucker. I only came to have him stabilized so we could go home and rest a little and then get back to throwing balls and swimming. That's all. Just that.

"You could leave him here and we could try to stabilize him, but I am afraid that you might be getting a phone call at 3 a.m."

I am shifting in my seat as I write this. It is coming back to me. The anxiety, the fear, the tears, the anger, the disbelief. Maybe that is why it has taken thirty-eight weeks to recount this.

"It is entirely possible that your dog will either suffer a cardiac arrest or go into complete respiratory failure. When they get to the stage he is in, the panting represents his attempt to get oxygen. And the more he tries to get oxygen, the more strain it puts on his heart. I can't tell you what to do, but humane euthanasia is an option at this point."

I ONLY BROUGHT HIM IN FOR STABILIZATION.

They say making the decision is hard. People always ask, "When will you know?" I always read those questions and inevitably, the answers are, "You will know" and "They will tell you." I doubted that until I didn't.

David and I looked at each other. We did not have to ask each other. Our eyes said it all.

"Okay, we will come back out to get you." In the eight weeks that Nubby-Bean was sick, I always noticed on the counter that when you checked in, there was a little fake candle and a sign that said, "Please monitor your voice. If this light is on, it means that somebody is saying their final goodbye." I always cried when I saw that sign, but never once did I really think it would pertain to me until it did.

I only came for stabilization. Tucky was standing up when we got into the room. While he did come to me, he was distracted. He was anxious. He couldn't settle. He was not my Nubby-Bean. His breathing had not improved. He had a line in his leg. *I have to stop writing now. I will come back whenever.*

"What is that?" He was standing up, clearly uncomfortable and ill at ease. He did not schnozzle me. He did not look that happy to see me. I wonder if he even knew if I was there. Could that be possible?

"It is a line that we will use to give him his sedative. He will go to sleep. He will not feel anything."

Maybe he won't feel anything, but the pain I was feeling was incomprehensible. Everything was pounding. My baby. My Tucker. My Nubby-Bean. My Lemon-Head. My everything.

The medicine took effect. He settled down. He lay on the

floor. I cradled his head. I cradled his body. I held him to me like he was one of my own. I whispered in his ear.

"He is sleeping now. He will feel nothing," they said as they pushed the medication that would stop his heart. My palm was flush against his chest, and I held him. I felt the rise and fall of his breathing until I didn't.

"Is he dead?" I asked.

She listened to her stethoscope. "He's at peace."

I died with him.

I buried my head into his fur. I held him tight. I told him that I loved him for his whole life. I told him that I would never forget him. I told him to rest in peace. My husband had to pull me away. Thirty-eight weeks later, as I write this, I feel the same anxiety and pain as I recount his last moments. I did not leave his side. I hope he knew I was there.

I am reading this eighty-one weeks later as I work with the editors. I died again just now, re-reading this. I died again just now, reliving the last moments. I died again. It never goes away.

I have never integrated politics into any of these posts, but today I have to. The governor of South Dakota killed her fourteen-month-old puppy named Cricket, with a gun, in a gravel pit, because she was what—having the time of her life? Messing up the hunt? Not listening? And let's not even talk about the goat she killed.

Whatever she was trying to say or whatever she thought

revealing that would bring to her politically is not my issue. My issue is YOU KILLED YOUR PUPPY. WHAT KIND OF MONSTER ARE YOU? If you do not want to train the dog, find a rescue. But to shoot a puppy in cold blood. This is not a partisan issue. You shot your puppy. Now compare that to John Stewart and his Dipper. His very public announcement of the pain he was feeling when they had to put their dog down. Losing a pet is the hardest thing to do. The grief comes and stays and hides and pops out. No warning. This is a particularly bad week as I think about how he will not be standing next to me with the blue ball when the pool people come.

Nubby-Bean, go find that Cricket and hug her tight. Let her know we love her even if her governor mom did not. Introduce her to the Chelse. They will get along. And give Bufie and Dex some treats.

Mama loves you More.

PS—I am not posting the pictures of our last goodbye. Even if one of the photos is just him sleeping, it is too hard and too painful, and I don't want to hurt anyone here. Instead, I am going to post happy times. And Cricket.

Yikes, I am interjecting here. Even though this text is a compilation of fifty-two weeks, one year, of grief, some of the interjections are being added post-fifty-two weeks. Some of the interjections are at seventy-one weeks, some at eight-one weeks since my Tucker left. And as I read these posts again as part of the process of publishing this journal, re-reading that one about his last moment gave me the same knock in my belly that it did when I was on the floor at the back of the hospital room. Now, I am eighty-one weeks past the initial grief. Yes, it has gotten easier. Yes, my life continues, but the pain of his passing, and recounting it here, still hurts. So, I will tell you that if you expect your grief to go away, it does not. If you expect to fully get over the loss, you will not. But you will find respite and it will ease.

WEEK 39

Let's talk for a moment. It's Tuesday, May 7. Last night, my youngest daughter gave birth to a beautiful baby girl. She has an incredible almost-three-year-old son who is filled with light and joy. My oldest daughter has two daughters. Are you old enough to remember the theme song from the *Patty Duke Show*? It was about two cousins. They were "identical bookends as different as night and day." That describes my two granddaughters. And my middle daughter has a son whose excitement and happiness with the world around him is a delight to see. All beautiful children, all very different.

As you can see, I have three daughters. I love them all, and they are all different. Not once did I ever feel that having another child was disloyal to the first child or the second child. Not once did I ever feel the second child or the third was replacing something that was missing in any of the previous children. Not once did I ever feel anything but love for all three of my children.

When my mother died, the grief was unbearable. A fifteen-year-old girl without her mother. Who was going to help me navigate those blossoming teenage years? But time does pass, and my life grew around the grief. Another wonderful woman came into my dad's life and subsequently into mine. The bond and our love grew. And while the grief over losing my birth mother still lived within, Trudy softened it with her devotion. And when she died, grief returned. Like a cake, another layer was added. But time does pass, and my life grew around the grief. And my father found love again.

The two of them are still together, going on for over twenty-three years. He is going to be ninety-nine, and she is going to be one hundred. They, too, have had their share of grief over the years, or should I say decades. But time does pass, and their lives grew around the grief.

Today is Wednesday, May 8. My daughter came home from the hospital and introduced the new baby to her son, who is just shy of three. The look on his face as he studied the baby was one of complete wonderment that brought tears to both my eyes and my daughter's eyes. "I love you," he said to his little baby sister. My daughter had tears of joy as she sat there and watched how her life had changed again. A growing family. Yes, there will be trials and tribulations as they grow into a family of four, but they will be filled with love, devotion, and gratitude. First you are a couple, then a family of three, and now a family of four. It is the natural order of things. Because time passes and life grows.

I have chosen the memorial items. The jar of blue racquetballs. Nothing says Tucker more than the blue rubber balls. Ball is life.

Tucker's head was a perfect little oval. It reminded me of the shape of a lemon. And so one of his long-term nicknames was born: Lemon-Head. Did you know there is actually a candy named Lemonheads? I did not. The candy was launched in 1962,

Tucker's name launched in 2016. When I saw the box of candy on the grocery store shelf, I had to have it.

There are hundreds of photos. Maybe more. But again, which ones are the most Tuckerish? We have a recliner. Tucker liked to jump up on my lap when I sat on it. He would often rest his head and schnozzle on the arm of the chair. Another little oddity was Tucker's reaction to the voice of the GPS service, Waze. Whenever he would hear the voice say, "All set, let's go," he would immediately stop whatever he was doing and come and jump up and sit on my lap. He enjoyed it so much that it took on a name forever etched in my vocabulary. Tucker-Time. Tucker-Time chair photo earns a coveted position.

My little native dog of South Carolina loved the snow. He would bury his schnozzle in the drifts and eat the snow, and then he would run out over the rocks and small mounds of what we called the back forty. That wonderful photo of my carefree snow dog enjoying life in the New England winter will occupy another coveted spot.

Swimming. Watch out. The pool belongs to Tucker. From early morning to night, if you threw the ball, he was in it. And when he was hot and needed to rest, he buried himself in the cool dirt under the bushes. And Tucker-of-the-Jungle was born.

Namaste and meditation were practices that Tucker engaged in. I have a tendency to anthropomorphize Nubby-Bean. I think mediation is a practice he engaged in even if dogs do not know that is what they do. He would hop onto the couch with his favorite gray Wubba bunny. He would hold it in his mouth and slowly begin to close his eyes, lapsing into a silent meditative state, his paws making biscuits on the Wubba as he self-regulated and calmed himself. It is hard to capture life in photos, but it serves its purpose to remind you of and reawaken your memories of the good.

And of course, my beautiful stained-glass portrait of Tucker-Ridge as a puppy and as a grown boy. Thank you, Colleen Kearns Hendricks, for creating the most beautiful forever memento that most certainly has gained a place of prominence. And last but not at all least, Kim Orsini, you have created, with love and the never-ending devotion of the Boykin Nation, a beautiful, peaceful resting place for my Nubby-Bean.

And just now, on Friday, May 10, thirty-nine weeks past his passing, David and I unpacked the Cornell bag. For the first time, I read the loving sympathy card from the caring staff at Cornell. What a tough job they have. His beautiful paw print is forever etched in a case. The paws that ran around and gave me high fives when I asked. The paws whose nails I was afraid to cut because I did not want to hurt him. They are there, and it will remind me of him.

The tin came out. I stared at it. The tears welled. I opened it. I took out the bag of ashes. They were heavy and white. I touched the bag. In my mind's eye, I thought it would be brown, like his beautiful Boykin Brown. I did not think of the reality of what color it would actually be due to the cremation process. My next immediate thought was, "How could that be my Tucker? My boy in a bag? How could that be my Nubby-Bean?" I turned to David and cried as we placed his remains in his final resting place. "Rest in peace, Tucker," I said.

It was a cleansing cry, and I said, "I really loved him. A whole lot." And David responded, tears in his own eyes, "I know. I did, too." But the truth is that he isn't in that urn. He is inside me. In my memories, in the love we shared, in the joy we gave each other. Every time I think of him and his funny ways, I will remember how we were a family. A family whose love was strong and whose grief is strong.

The past thirty-nine weeks have taught me a lot about love, grief, friendship, and gratitude. Nubby-Bean, your place in my heart is secure. And should another beautiful Boykin enter my life to give and receive love, it will in no way diminish who you were and are. It will in no way diminish my love for you because, like children and grandchildren, everyone is different and deserving of love. No one is a replacement. Part of the world's wonder.

Nubby-Bean, you live in my heart every day. Thirty-nine weeks. Time goes on, and my life grows around the grief. The acceptance is still growing. I miss you every single day. Lemon-Head. You know the drill. Kiss Tootsie Roll Buster, hug the Chelse. Kiss Cricket. Say hi to Bufie and Dex. Oh, and tell them that in every book so far, they are always getting treats. I will let you know when the books are out.

Love you more,

Mama

WEEK 40

Last week, I found the courage to create Tucker's memorial. I had returned home from helping my daughter, who had just given birth. A new life, a new beginning. I woke up the following morning. I told David, "Come, it's time. It's time to take Tucker's remains and create his memorial." And if you read the posts, I discussed the process. I am not completely certain of what dynamic played out that allowed me to take the leap, but I believe part of it was watching a new life being born. To share a very overused phrase but an appropriate one made famous by Mufasa in *The Lion King*, it is the circle of life. People are born and people die. Joni Mitchell herself coined this dynamic when she wrote these words in her song "The Circle Game" (1966):

> *And the seasons they go round and round*
> *And the painted ponies go up and down*
> *We're captive on the carousel of time*
> *We can't return, we can only look behind*
> *From where we came*
> *And go round and round and round*
> *In the circle game.*

It is the way things work.

Creating the memorial was also a function of another age-old adage, "time heals all wounds." Have you ever thought about that phrase? I understand the truth of that phrase. I have lost many people who I loved and still love, but time has eased the pain. Time has softened the blow. Time has made it easier to live with my grief. Time does not erase your memories. Time does not take your loss away. Time just changes your perspective. Time lets you take a deep breath and move on.

I knew I needed to put Tucker's memorial together so I could let him rest in peace. That is another phrase that is often used. And it is a phrase designed for the mourner, not the one who passed. Tucker does not know he is resting in peace. It is a phrase that is designed to let the mourner begin to heal. It is a phrase that is designed to allow the mourner to accept the loss and deal with the many emotions that losing someone you love brings on. And when emotions are recognized and handled, life proceeds.

I am approaching a tough season. I am approaching the moment in time when we were blindsided by a diagnosis we did not see coming. I am approaching the moment in time when we realized the word "terminal" was something other than a bus or train or airplane building. I am approaching the moment in time when uncertainty, fear, and anticipatory grief become my constant companion. I am approaching the moment in time when I would lie awake at night and impatiently wait for daylight, and then I would anxiously wait for the day to end and the night to begin. I am approaching the moment in time when the ticking of the clock and the passing of the days were daggers. And in the not-too-distant future, I am approaching the moment in time when I had to say goodbye.

I can honestly say that last summer was by far the worst summer I ever had. And no matter how bad things could get, this summer will be better because life goes on; it grows around the grief. And so, I will continue to work through those difficult times that are coming my way because I still believe that my writing helps me heal, and hopefully, it will continue to help others.

For those of you who follow my weeks of threads, The Reaper Plant is moving outside.

Nubs, it is forty weeks. I miss you and think about you all the time. I know how happy you would be now as the weather warms. Tucker-Ridge, I owe you a letter. Next week, I will fill you in. Please kiss Tootsie Roll Buster and Cricket. Give the Bufe and Dex treats and hug the Chelse. Book's not out yet, but I will let you know.

Love you even more,

Mama

WEEK 41

Dear Nubby-Bean,

I promised you a letter, and I have been meaning to talk with you for a while now. Nubby, you know the bridge in the backyard? I know you remember it. Well, when the little girls come to sleep over, I still talk about that bridge in their bedtime stories. You remember the stories revolve around all the family dogs who gather around and play. And then, all of a sudden, a unicorn appears, crossing the bridge. The unicorn tells all the doggos they are going to go to Unicorn Land. In Unicorn Land, the clouds are soft beds, the flowers taste like their favorite treats, the pools are filled with whatever you like to drink, and it rains bully sticks. And when you crossed the Rainbow Bridge and Buster left us, the story morphed. And now, of course, all the doggies cross the UNICORN Bridge to see you. It is a childhood pleasure to pretend they are seeing their fur families again.

Not long after you died, I decided that I was going to turn that bridge, the one you used to run across with your ball, into our very own personal Unicorn Rainbow Bridge. I was going to start it in the fall, but Dada said to wait until the spring because the leaves were starting to fall and he thought the leaves would ruin the paint. He was right, but it seemed so long to wait. But it is getting warmer so I will be able to do it soon. Here is what it is going to look like. All the boards are going to be painted in rainbow colors. And then on each plank are the names of all our babies who are with you now. You, of course, Tucker, Nubby-Bean, and Tootsie Roll Buster, the Chelse, Dex, the Bufe, Owen's Oreo, Amy's Phoebe, Amanda's Bodhi, and Cricket. I know Cricket did not live with us, but she met such a sad and mean end that she deserves to have a place of love on our Rainbow Bridge. And then, because the girls love unicorns, there will be unicorns and all kinds of rainbow designs. I added a picture of the bridge, the way it looks now, the way you remember it. I even added a picture of you running across the bridge with that favored blue racquetball.

I think it is going to be a wonderful place to visit. I think it will bring many of us hope and joy. We can come out to the bridge, stand on it, and feel every one of our fur babies' love. It will be a mystical place. It will be a remembrance place. It will be a place of comfort and solace, at least that is what I think. What do you think?

Today, when I was wandering the yard, I heard a little croaking sound. And do you know what I heard, Tucker? Frogs. I took a closer look, and there were four of them living in the puddles on the pool cover. The water was a little bit dirty from the winter, and I could not really see the whole frog. But when I got closer to the side of the pool, I noticed beady little eyes peeking out. And oh, Tucker, I started to laugh because I remember how, when you saw a frog in the pool, and in you would go try to catch it. It was the only thing that could distract you from your ball. Then, when you would jump in, the frog would dive to the bottom, and you would get so mad! Well, that would go on for a long time, and we would finally have to leave the frog. But later, I would make sure the frog got out of the pool because I did not want the chlorine to hurt it. The next morning when we got outside, the first thing you did, do you remember? The first thing you would do is run to the pool and stand there by its side, searching for the frog. You remembered! You had such a good memory. And I would laugh and laugh. And finally, I would say, "He's gone Nubby-Bean. Go get your ball."

And right next to the pool, as I walked around, I saw the fronds of the Tucker-of-the-Jungle plant. Turning green as the weather warms, its fronds starting to grow, I peeked under the bottom fronds, and while I knew you were not cooling yourself there, I peeked under the bottom fronds because that was your place to go when it was hot and you wanted to cool yourself. Your body hidden deep inside green blades, your head and schnozzle sticking out. Oh, Nubby-Bean, how cute you were lying there in your little paradise. Tucker-of-the-Jungle, you would lie there until something else suddenly grabbed your attention. And then, Lemon-Head, out you would dart to chase whatever was intriguing you. It was funny to watch you dart out. Maybe I will put one of the Cuddle Clones under the plant and send it to you. You can then tell me whether or not the Clone looks enough like you that you have to do a double-take like I did the first time I saw the clone in Tucky's Bed or on our Tucker-Time chair. Will you do that for me? Will you let me know if you think the Clone looks enough like you? I know you live in my heart and my mind, but sometimes, seeing that little clone in the morning, when I am still sleepy and a bit unclear…it feels like you are here.

I have a few other things I have to tell you, Tucker. I was visiting the grandgirls this week like I do every week. And in one of the conversations I had with Nani (she is going to be a character in one of the Nubby-Bean books), she said she misses you. We were doing homework, and her comment just came right out. She said that she really misses her Buster, or the Bus, and she then said she misses you. She said she knew you made us all so happy, and she loved to watch you dance and walk backward for your cookie. She said it was funny when you came upstairs to the bathtub and tried to drink the water and got bubbles on your nose. She said she missed you, and I think both of us got tears in our eyes.

So, you see, Nubby-Bean, even though you are not physically here with us, your memory is. And we all miss you. When we all think of you, we cry, but we also remember all your funnies. And remembering those funnies makes everyone happy. It is going to be hot this weekend, Nubby-Bean. I hope you are going to have a good time this Memorial Day Weekend. I will remember your memory this weekend. And Dex, and the Buster, and Bufie, Cricket, and the Chelse.

I will keep you posted on all the different things that happen this weekend, Nubby-Bean. You know the drill. Give a kiss. And yes,

Love you more,

Mama

WEEK 42

We are ten weeks out from reaching a year that you have been gone. I say that out loud and go, "Whoa." How can that be? So much has happened. I wrote about the passage of time in many of my earlier writings. I wrote about how time seems to stand still and then fly at the same time. I wrote about how time hurts and stabs but also soothes.

Time is a human invention. The passage of time is not marked by the seasons. We mark the seasons as passages of time. We mark time to put some sort of order into our lives. Time is not a fixed piece of reality, but it is a continuum of a sequenced form of existence. It measures what came before, what is happening now, what may be in the future. But even that is relative. There is a very interesting book written by Alan Lightman titled *Einstein's Dream*. It is short and fascinating. It looks at different scenarios of time as devised by a young Einstein. It looks at what time would be like, what life would be like, if we knew time in a different way. Read it. It is how I feel at times as I think about the passage of time.

I am approaching my seventieth year. What? Really? How in God's name did that happen? Where did the time go? My dad is approaching his ninety-ninth year. Really? How did that happen? I am lucky. I have had my daddy in my life for a very long time, and I still cherish every single moment we have together. But ninety-nine years. It is amazing what he has seen and witnessed. My littlest granddaughter is only one month old. She will be experiencing the wonders of early adulthood when I will be but a memory. Really? How did that happen?

My children, whose knees I bandaged, whose tears I dried, are now bandaging the knees and wiping the eyes of their children. Time has taken my children, who loved Sesame Street and bumper cars, and put them in roles that are fraught with good times and worries. In a nutshell, time has made them parents. They will have to make the decisions that will guide their lives and the lives of their children. I am no longer the mommy. Sometimes, when I think of that, I go wait—what? How did that happen? I have had to take a step back and adapt to a new role because time has shifted the goalposts, and my world has changed. Time is limited. Use it wisely.

The Byrds pegged it in their song "Turn! Turn! Turn!" (1965):

To everything turn, turn, turn
There is a season turn, turn, turn
And a time to every purpose under Heaven
A time to be born, a time to die
A time to plant, a time to reap
A time to kill, a time to heal
A time to laugh, a time to weep.

And there are many more verses to this tune, indicating

just how common the questions about time are. Time is what you make of it. Tucker, forty-two weeks of time have passed. I think of you daily. It is easier. Yes, there are times when your loss strikes me in the gut and I feel it like it was day one, but more often than not, when I think of you, I think of how lucky I was to have you as my boy. I look at your memorial, and I smile. I talk about you with joy.

The Unicorn Rainbow Bridge is under construction. And the first children's book about you is in its final stages. Tucker-Ridge, Dad went to visit his mom's final resting place, and he saw a site with the name Tucker's Ridge on it. Take a look at that, too. There are so many reminders of you. And the passage of time has allowed me to see many of these beautiful reminders rather than sharp-edged, caustic triggers that create pain. I suppose one of the things I want to say is that grief is one of those things that you have to go through to get through. Everyone's time frame is different. Everyone's grief journey is different. Everyone's constitution and tolerance level are different. We are all different, yet we are all united in our need for time to help us come to terms with our lives, the passage of time, and our journeys through the ups and downs of our existence.

Nubby-Bean, go kiss and hug all the best boys and girls up there. We miss the Chelse, Bufe, and Dex. We think about all of you and Tootsie Roll Buster. Mama will keep you posted on the bridge and the books.

Love you so much more,
Mama

WEEK 43

Just about a year ago, we were in the midst of planning a large family celebration. We had been trying to have a "significant" number birthday party for David, but COVID and its variants kept getting in the way. I think I was sending more Evite cancellations than anything else. But finally, in June 2023, it looked like the party was on. Seventy-plus, but then, since Dad was going to turn ninety-eight during the summer, we decided to celebrate his birthday as well because you can't always trust time.

I hired a caterer. I planted colorful plants in pots. I picked a color scheme and bought tablecloths and nice outdoor dishes. Beautiful pitchers, and, well, everything else that would create a beautiful environment. The party was going to be held on a Sunday afternoon in early June. It wouldn't be too hot, it wouldn't interfere with summer vacations, and there were several family members who lived across the country who were actually on the East Coast.

And just about a year ago, at the same time, I noticed that Tucker did not seem himself. I won't rehash a lot of what I noticed because I have already done that—a lot—so in between phone calls with the caterer and visits to HomeGoods, I took him to his vet. I left him there because he had a fever and his eyes did not look good. In fact, his beautiful, yellow Boykin eyes were blood red. She called a few hours later and told me to come and get him, and when I did, she told me that she was not happy with his X-ray, which showed an enlarged spleen. She wanted an ultrasound done and told me to take him to MedVet hospital. They were expecting us.

I felt nausea rise up. The enlarged spleen was a trigger. My mother had an enlarged spleen. She died six weeks later of cancer. The vet watched as the color blanched from my face and told me it did not mean cancer. Many tick-borne diseases cause enlarged spleens, and she gave me a dosage of doxycycline. The MedVet hospital was very clinical and quiet. Not at all like our vet's friendly office, whose walls are covered with the "patients" pictures. Tucker still holds two places on the wall. On the desk at MedVet, there was a sign that brought tears to my eyes when I read it. It said:

If the light is on, someone is saying goodbye to their beloved pet. We ask that you speak softly during this difficult time. Thank you for your kindness and compassion.

How sad, I thought, but I never really thought it would apply to me.

They brought Tucker in, and he came out with a shaved belly. That was a little bit of a shocker. They gave him a treat, and we left. I was concerned, but truth be told, I wasn't really worried yet. We live in a woody area. Our backyard is filled with rocks and trees and water. Yes, we spray, but he had had canine anaplasmosis before, so I was fairly certain that was going to be the diagnosis. I went home, and we prepped for the party.

The party was wonderful. Friends, family, good wishes, a real celebration. Tucker was a bit subdued, but we had also given him some trazodone to calm him for the party because we did not want him to be overstimulated by all the people. And he loved people. He also loved to jump on them. And just about a year ago, the day after the party, we were sitting in the house with some visiting cousins, talking about how fun the party was, when a phone call came in from MedVet.

"We have been trying to reach you. We left several messages."

I checked my phone. "Oh, I just checked my phone, and I do not see any messages or a missed call. Although I may have deleted it if I did not recognize the number."

"Well, Tucker's FNA biopsy came back, and it is consistent with lymphoma."

"WHAT? What! What do you mean?"

"Blah, blah, blah, blah, blah, blah, Blah, blah, blah, blah, blah, blah. You should try to get an appointment with an oncologist right away because lymphoma can be aggressive, depending on its type."

And just about a year ago, the summer of 2023, or the summer of hell, as I "fondly" refer to it, began. And again, I will not delve into the details. They have been duly documented over the past forty-three weeks, but what I do want to talk about are the hopes I have for the summer of 2024.

Good things have happened in the past year. A new grandchild has been born. My father is still healthy—for a soon-to-be ninety-nine-year-old. My stepmom is right alongside him, boasting a mere 100 years in September. All good. And I know this might be hard to read, and it is actually hard to write, but some good things have happened since Tucker left me. My grief has allowed me to become more introspective about what grief means to me and how it has affected me. I learned things. Maybe I learned things that I would not have learned if I had not lost my best boy.

I became a writer with the goal of helping others. If my writing has helped others get in touch with their own personal grief journey, then I have to thank my Nubby-Bean. If my writing has helped others see there is healing (even though I did not believe those people who, just about a year ago, said there was), then good.

The pool is open. Yes, when the cover came off, and I saw the water, I visualized Nubby-Bean there even though he was not. The Reaper Plant is back outside and is coming back. It is living in a pot with newer plants, ones that I just planted. They are not the same plant as the Reaper. But they are together. The Unicorn Rainbow Bridge is almost done, but the weather has not been cooperating, so I have been unable to finish it. But Nubby-Bean, like your memory and Dex's, Bufe's, the Chelsea's, and Tootsie Roll Buster's, it is not going away and will still be here for me to finish.

Nubby-Bean, things still happen around here. They happen without you, but they happen. Still think of you every single day, more than once. And I smile about how lucky I was to have you as my very special boy.

And, for sure, you know what to do now with our friends up there.

I love you even more than that!

Mama

WEEK 44

Wednesday was my wedding anniversary. It was also the one-year mark that we got Tucker's lymphoma diagnosis. I think you all know it was a hard summer last year. I think you all know my stance on anticipatory grief. I think you all know there are still days, many days, when I feel Tucker's presence and lack thereof. I think you all know I have been writing every week to help me on my grief journey and hopefully help you. I think you all know I loved my Nubby-Bean more than I ever thought possible. I see him now when I look at the Unicorn Rainbow Bridge. I see him when I think about him. He was my best boy. He still is.

Tucker's life with us gave us eight great years. His life with us was in the physical past. I am not going to get metaphysical. So now I want to talk about the present.

There is so much new here. There is a new baby in the family. My daughter and son-in-law have a brand-new little girl just starting her journey. She is a blank slate. She is innocent and open and surrounded by a loving family who will move the earth to make sure she grows up happy, healthy, and secure. Hopefully, she will learn to trust the people in her world and view the world as a place of magic and hope. She has an older brother who looks at her with marvel. "She's so little." Here's to his new role as a protective brother who will learn to adapt to his own growing family and the importance of his role as he grows himself. He is surrounded by a loving family who will move the earth to make sure he grows up happy, healthy, and secure. Hopefully, he will learn to trust the people in his world and view the world as a place of magic and hope. Here's to hoping that the troubles and weight of the world don't touch them for as long as humanly possible.

There is a new home for another daughter and son-in-law. Their growing family is moving from an environment that served them well as a couple, but as a growing family, their needs moved from meeting their own individual needs to those of two growing children. As they enter this new phase, they will accept all the challenges with love and gusto. Two growing children who will begin their lives in a new place, a place that will be theirs and provide the security that a loving home brings. With their loving family, who is there to support them through all that comes their way, hopefully, they will grow up happy and secure and develop into the very best people they can be.

I had my anniversary this week. I continue to appreciate my life with David every single day. Together, we have built a happy and fulfilling life more than I ever thought possible. We both started over. We both found love again, and our love has grown for our combined families. Together, we have five children, and now we have seven grandchildren. Together, we have four sons-in-law, and along with them, an extended family we find joy in. We adore them all and take such pleasure in watching them grow and learn how to be parents and guide their beautiful children. Here is to hoping that they will all make the best of each day and love the world as we love them.

My father is two months shy of turning ninety-nine, and my stepmom is about two and one-half months shy of turning 100. Yes, they have seen the troubles and the weight of the world from family problems, illnesses, and multiple wars. But they are managing to live and find what enjoyment they can. If the fact that they are still here makes me happy, then I hope that alone will keep them happy because they are truly surrounded by a loving family who will move the earth to make sure they continue to be healthy, happy, and secure. They certainly know that the troubles of the world are many, but they also know that the strength of the human spirit can guide and direct life so that love can always prevail. And here's to hoping that the troubles and weight of the world don't touch them anymore for as long as humanly possible.

Tucker, we did everything we could to keep you happy, healthy, and secure. Your happiness was our happiness. Your joy was our joy. Your Tuckerisms made us laugh. Whether it was talking to your bone, staring at your ball, meditating with your Wubba bunny, begging for treats, running away from the voice of the Waze GPS, or simply sitting on my lap for Tucker-time, you were surrounded by a loving family who DID MOVE the earth to make sure that you stayed as healthy, happy, and secure as you could be. And yes, I believe that you did view the world as a place of magic and hope. There was always the hope of a new marrow bone when I came home from the store. There was always the hope of a new blue racquetball when the box from Amazon was opened. There was always the hope of a treat or a bully stick or a swim. There was always love, Nubby-Bean, and know that when the troubles and the weight of the lymphoma world were too much to bear, we continued to surround you with love and let you go peacefully so that you would not have to deal with the troubles and weight of the world. We kept you for as long as humanly possible. You know the drill. Nubby-Bean, kiss the Chelse, Bufie and Dex, Tootsie Roll Buster, and that wonderful Cricket. And please introduce yourself to Phoebe and Riley-Roo and Piper.

I love you more,

Mama

WEEK 45

I do not know where the week went. Usually, the minute I post, my ideas for the following week come rumbling right up to the surface. Not so much this week. This week, there were many other human issues to deal with. Issues with children and grandchildren. Issues with elderly parents. So, suddenly, I found myself, just yesterday, able to think about what I wanted to share with you. When I started this grief journey, I did not think there would ever be another happy day. I did not think there would ever be a day where I could smile or think positive thoughts. I did not think there would ever be a day where my thinking about Tucker would not leave me crippled. And in the many posts that I read in the beginning, I read with disbelief when others said it gets better, it eases; you don't forget, but you survive, and on and on and on. "Maybe for you," I thought, "but not for me." My love for my Nubby-Bean was too deep for the pain to ever go away. Well, for those of you whose posts I have read and internally felt you were being untruthful, I am sorry because you were right. And for those of you just entering this incredibly hurtful journey, it does ease. Let me explain.

It is summer here in New England. And this was Tucker's favorite season. He would spend hours and hours chasing those famous blue racquetballs, swimming, chasing the frogs, eating ice cubes, and simply sitting at the top of the deck steps looking out over his territory, watching for any movement at all. A chipmunk, a squirrel, a frog, a bunny, a bird, and when his keen eyes saw the movement, off he would go. Watching him chase the squirrels was often enjoyable. They were too fast and there were too many trees in the yard. Down the steps he would go, and up into the tree the squirrel would go. He would stand at the bottom of the trunk and bark at it, but then he would return to the deck. What I loved was his persistence, his dedication, and his perseverance—three traits that Olympic athletes need. He never got depressed, he never felt like a failure; he simply waited for the next bird or squirrel or frog and tried again. What a lesson my Tucky taught me. Don't give up, keep trying, the only failure is not trying. You lose all of those.

Yesterday, I was sitting outside, and I saw a really big frog on the outside of the pool. I saw a squirrel run across the lawn, and instead of crying, I simply said to myself, "Wow, Tucker would have jumped up and been all over those two, trying the best he could to catch them." I got wistful, but I also felt happy about how I had that experience.

When the heat of yesterday got to me and I got in the pool, I thought about how the minute I got in would have been a clear signal to Tucker-Ridge to go get his ball and drop it in the water so I could throw it. It is true I missed that, but in its absence, I was able to simply float for a few minutes by myself. It did not mean that I did not miss him, but I was able to take a few moments for myself. That does not mean I do not miss him; it means that I am learning to live my life without him near me. I think the concept of having to learn how to live your life without your dog is understandable by all who KNOW and maybe not understandable by those who DON'T. If your life has never been graced by the presence of a special dog, you might not understand the depth of grief and the struggle to recover. I am recovering. Take a look at Jon Stewart's video of the loss of his best boy Dipper, when he wishes for all people to go and find that one dog…

You can find it on YouTube. As soon as you type in Jon Stewart, it comes right up. If you know, you will need a tissue. If you don't know, you might be able to get a glimpse.

But healing does occur. It has been forty-five weeks since my heart fell out of my body and the explosion of grief crippled me. It has been forty-five weeks since I shook my head in disbelief and wondered how this could be happening to me, how this could be my life, and forty-five weeks since I got invited to the biggest pity party on the planet. But it is also forty-five weeks of healing and realizing that on this planet, in this realm, animals are mortal and they leave their earthly life, and no amount of wishing on a broken wishbone or a star or closing your eyes and blowing out the candles will bring them back. So, you adjust and learn to keep them alive with your memories and your thoughts.

And you know what else? What else is that I now find that the better memories, the happy ones of my Nubby-Bean, are outnumbering the bad ones because what I want to remember is the catatonic look of joy that came across his eyes when he was eating a pup ice cream instead of the fearful look in his eyes every time we entered Cornell. I want to remember the smile that crossed my face when he jumped up and caught the ball instead of the frown I wore when looking at the shaved legs where IV needles were inserted. And I want to remember the sheer joy when he saw us come into the house instead of the confused and agitated boy he was on his last day when his breathing was labored. And you know what? I am beginning to be able to do that.

The Unicorn Rainbow Bridge is almost done. My first book is headed to publication. My Nubby-Bean will live on in the pages of the books I am writing and hopefully will give hope to all who are dealing with the hardships of life.

Nubby-Bean. Hang out with Oreo and Cricket. Kiss the Chelse. Say hi to Tootsie Roll Buster. Be the best to Bufie and Dex. Don't forget Phoebe. Go swimming. It is hot outside.

Love you even more.

Mama

WEEK 46

Summer is in full swing. The first heat wave has come and gone. July Fourth is around the corner, which means that, before you know it, it is Labor Day. Yesterday, I saw a back-to-school ad for Staples. The school I work in is not out yet. It is an extended-year school for mostly urban children who need more assistance. I am not going to talk about rushing our lives because I already did that in a previous post. I am not going to talk about whether or not you think time is a thief or a friend because I have done that already, too. I might decide to talk about something entirely different, but we will see where this goes.

I want to say that one year ago, this week, was the first of many disappointing moments when we were told the chemo was not working on Tucker. It was always a stab in the heart when we heard that, and we heard that all the time. I know how all of you feel if you are getting that news and living with that dynamic. From the outset, if you are dealing with canine lymphoma, you are dealing with a terminal illness. Some of you may get long remissions, some of you may not. I did not. It is a roulette wheel. Some of you will win, and some of you will lose.

I do not miss last summer. It was a daily pull on my heart and my stomach. It was a daily struggle to get up and keep up a happy face. But I knew that as long as I could get up and throw the ball to a Tucker who would chase it, it was my job to do so. So, for all of you who are living the dynamic of getting up in the morning and trying to find the strength to enjoy each precious moment, I know how you feel. Some of you will be able to do it easily, some of you will not.

Last summer, I spent a good deal of time looking at Nubby-Bean's shaved legs and wondering what color stretchy wrap would be on his leg when he came out of the office at Cornell. If you could remove the reason for the shaved legs, you might almost be able to laugh at his furry body juxtaposed against his skinny little legs, but I couldn't, and I do not miss looking at that. Some of you are looking at those legs right now, and if you are, I know how you feel. Some of you might not be looking at those shaved legs yet, and if you're not, thank God, and if you will be shortly, I know how you feel.

Last summer, I could not wait to close the pool. I could not stand to look at it. It was naked and empty. It was a trigger. I did not want to look at it without him in it. Last fall, I walked through the New England fall leaves without him jumping into the leaves and coming out of the piles with leaves stuck in his fur. Last year, we did a lot of things that we did not do this year, but the pain of the NOT-DOING has lessened. It lessened with acceptance. There is something very true about the stages of grief. Do you know what they are? Denial, anger, bargaining, depression, and acceptance. Now, remember, these stages are not as linear as they look. Their boundaries and borders are soft and flexible. As I have said, grief is a private journey with no timeline.

You purchased a one-way ticket and have no idea when your return flight is or how much it is going to cost. Sort of like a timeshare you want to get out of but can't. I realize even with an increasing level of acceptance, there is still sadness. I miss him, but I am not bargaining anymore. I am saving my bargaining for street vendors who are asking way too much money for the cheap goods they are selling on the street. I have a daughter who is so good at bargaining that I heard her once say to a street vendor, "You should pay me to take that pocketbook away. That's how junky it is." He lowered the price. I am beyond denial because, hey, he is not here. I can't deny the fact that he got sick and left the fambily sooner than we would have liked. Anger? Sometimes, but really, what good is it going to do to be angry? Whom am I going to be angry with? Some Almighty that I do not really subscribe to? Some power or fate? Nope. I can dislike the situation, which I did and still do, but anger is a wasted emotion. It isn't going to make me feel better or make the facts change, so I have learned to let it go.

What is the point of all this? The point of all this is that healing is occurring. And for all of you who think you will never heal, like I thought, you will. It won't be smooth, but it will happen. It is like repairing a piece of broken china. You use invisible glue and hold the two pieces of the china together until the Super Glue takes hold. You rub off the remnants, and your plate is ready to use again. You can fill it with pasta or salad. It can reappear on your Thanksgiving table, and it will do just fine. And if you look at it, it looks just fine, but if you study it carefully, there is that tiny little crack line. That is healing. Your heart has that tiny little crack line. Sometimes it expands a little and the hurt and pain are stronger, and sometimes it recedes and you do not feel the pain and hurt as much. So for all of you going through whatever stage you are in, I understand how you feel.

Finding an understanding ear and someone to talk to is important. I hope my journey is helping you. Hey Nubby-Bean, my website for healing and my books are coming up. It is going to be called sheilacoopermanbooks.com. I hope the writing will help others. And some of the books, too, will be there next week. Nubby-Bean, tell Bufie and Dex that they keep asking for treats in the books and they are getting a little chunky. Run across the bridge a few times. And Chelsea, kiss her. How are Oreo and Phoebe? Did you run with them yet? And don't forget Cricket and Tootsie Roll Buster.

Dotticles says hi. Check out The Reaper Plant. It is back and thriving. Forty-six weeks, Tucker-Ridge. It feels like a lifetime, but it also feels like yesterday.

Love you more,
Mama

WEEK 47

It is just a few short weeks away until I mark the one-year anniversary (angelversary?) of Tucker's passing. It is hard to believe that almost a year of life has come and gone. As I look back on the year's grief journey, there are some things that have gotten easier and some things that I know will always be with me. That is not a bad thing because the truth is once you have experienced a love that brings such grief, it stays with you. It becomes part of who you are, part of your lived experience, part of you. I have respect for Friedrich Nietzsche's famous quote, "That which does not kill us makes us stronger." Even though it may not feel that way at the point of loss, I do believe it is true. I am getting through this loss. I do not lose my breath as often as I did. I can think about him and smile without getting that stomach stab.

At first, one of the things I did to try to keep Tucker in my life was to collect as many Boykin-related things as possible. Here is an inventory: five Boykin-looking statues that I bought at various Marshalls and TJ Maxx stores. I painted them brown and colored the eyes yellow. Boykin dish towels. Boykin mugs. I have Boykin crocheted stuffies, Boykin T-shirts, Boykin sweatshirts. I have a beautiful stained-glass portrait made by Colleen at the

Glass Pansy. I have Boykin-looking bookends. I had two beautiful urns crafted. One holds his remains, and the other holds treats for all visiting pups. I have several great things from the OLBD (Operation Little Brown Dog) auctions. A beautiful tray, pieces of wood-carved art, a Boykin-inspired checkbook cover, and two Cuddle Clones. A beautiful memorial to my boy containing his paw prints, his favorite blue racquetballs, and a box of Lemonhead candies because one of my nicknames for him was Lemon-Head. Photos, photos, and more photos. Boykin this, Boykin that. And yes, I love it all, but the motivation behind all those purchases was to keep my Tucker alive. Maybe it was to pretend that he still was. But what I have learned is that no physical items will replace the best part of remembering him because he lives in my heart and my mind.

I started writing last year when we began our cancer journey. I found that writing helped me process all the ups and downs and roller coasters of emotions. It gave me a place to voice my angst, my fears, my hopes. And as it turned out, apparently, it has been helping others, and I find that very soothing. It makes me feel like my own struggles are made easier because it is less isolating and I am not alone. And in a scary world, not feeling alone is very important.

If you have been following any of my posts over the past eleven months, you also know I have a bridge in my backyard. A bridge that I turned into a rainbow unicorn bridge that now hosts all the names of beloved fur babies that have crossed. I have always fantasized about the "reality" of the Rainbow Bridge, and I find it appealing. So when I started writing, I came up with a story idea about this dog, Nubby-Bean (a.k.a. Tucker), who comes back over the Rainbow Bridge to help a grieving family. He becomes the family angel as he brings joy and hope. And then, he reappears with the Rainbow Brigade to help a little boy who has to come to terms with a new sibling. Next stop, they travel to a little girl whose best friend moved away and is sad. And all because my Nubby-Bean left his earthly domain. He left, and the book series *The Rainbow Brigade* was born.

My Nubby-Bean brought great joy to my life and my world, and the fact that I have created a lasting memorial to his time with us gives me great joy. I hope it will bring others great joy and relief, too. Hopefully, you will be able to get some relief by accessing sheilacoopermanbooks.com, where you can see many posts that might help you in your grief journey.

Nubby-Bean, it has been forty-seven weeks since I held you and kissed you and told you to go peacefully into the night. It has been forty-seven weeks since I learned just how much your presence was so much a part of our lives. It has been forty-seven weeks since I threw you a ball, but it has also been forty-seven weeks of happiness knowing that you were mine and I was yours, and death will never take that away.

Nubby-Bean, the girls are coming today. We are going to play on the bridge. Send us a sign. Say hi to Tootsie Roll Buster and Dex. Don't forget Piper and Oreo, and Cricket. Get Bufie a treat and hug that sweet old Chelse. Kiss Phoebe.

Love you even more,

Mama

WEEK 48

In four weeks, Tucker will be gone for a year. In seven weeks, my dad will be ninety-nine years old. Tomorrow, my grandson will be three years old. Chaucer is known for this famous quote: "Time and tide wait for no man." He said it in 1395 in the prologue to *The Clerk's Tale*. It is as true in 2024 as it was in 1395, a mere 629 years ago (though accounts differ on the date the book was actually written). Over the past forty-eight weeks, I have frequently written about time. It is both a thief and a savior. Sometimes you wish it would slow down, and sometimes you wish it would speed up. And maybe, sometimes, you wish it would just stop. Depends on the situation. Depends on your life and what is happening. Depends on your feelings.

I have written about how time is a human construct. We measure time so we can exert some sort of control over our lives and make some sense of where we are. We can't stop time. Whether we use a calendar or not, whether we look at a clock or not, time will pass and we will see its impact. We grow old. It is a fantasy, at times, to want to time travel or be able to change the time. After all, we manipulate time when we change the clocks. But when we do that, if you live in a state that does that, it upsets the circadian rhythms. Your dogs want that food, and they do not care what the clock says. The only way time can change, I suppose, is when you approach a black hole. I am not a physicist, but here it is: time can change. In addition to gravity stretching and squashing objects, another strange phenomenon that a traveler would observe close to a black hole is something called time dilation, in which time passes slower closer to the black hole than farther away. I do not know what that means, but if it would have made losing Tucker easier, I would have gone, if I could have, to a black hole.

Grieving is indeed personal. I am amazed at how I have grown. A year ago, I did not know if I would ever smile again. I did not know if I would ever be happy again. I did not know if I would find joy again. I loved my Tucker so much. And my life has been different without him. I still think about him every day. I still have his portrait and his leash and collar right next to my desk on the wall, and I look at them every day. I miss him and all his Tuckerisms.

But a year has just about passed. And just like in these lyrics from The Kid LAROI, "I Thought That I Needed You" (2023):

> *I never thought that I would find a way out*
> *I never thought I'd hear my heart beat so loud*
> *I can't believe there's something left in my chest anymore*
> *So many nights, my tears fell harder than rain*
> *Scared I would take my broken heart to the grave*
> *I'd rather die than have to live in a storm like before*
> *But it's time to love again.*

We went to see the lovely family that gave us Tucker. I admit, I was a bit nervous—well, actually scared—when I pulled into the driveway. I have not had any personal contact with a Boykin since Tucker died. I wondered how it would affect me to see so many Boykins that looked like my Nubby-Bean. Would I cry? Would I run away? Would I regret it? Would I feel like I was betraying Tucker's memory? When we entered the house, they were all there. Several grown Boykins as friendly as I remember my best boy being. Here was a new smell, me, and they all wanted a part of me. I sat down on the couch, and they all jumped up on me. I started giggling. But one dog got herself right onto my lap. It turned out that it was Tucker's mama. She schnozzled me like Tucker always did. She looked at me and I told her, "Tucker was a good boy. He was my best boy." I realized that I was ready to love again.

We went outside to the backyard and looked at all these little brown dogs and I could not stop smiling. Suddenly, I saw how much I missed having these little swamp poodles running around chasing sticks, eating bones, snuggling, and doing all the things they do. And I realized that I was ready to love again. All the doubt I had about ever loving again or ever having another dog again melted away. I was always skeptical about people who said the grief is bad, but it doesn't replace the joy. Ha, I thought. For you, maybe, but not for me. This grief will never go away. I could never do it again. And I believed that, and I meant it. But time has softened the blow. Over the weeks that I have been writing, I frequently post a picture of three jars with balls in them that represent how grief gets smaller and smaller, and more manageable, but it never completely goes away. What happens is life grows around it. It is true. You do not forget the grief. You don't want the grief, but it is part of the deal. It softens, I survived, I am surviving. It did not kill me. It changed me, but I made it. It took me a year to realize this. I have a good high school friend who told me last year that it took her a year to be able to breathe when her dog died. Joanie was right.

This new baby will be a different dog and a different love. He will have different "isms." He will have different quirks that will make us laugh. He will have different habits. He will have different sounds and different fears. He will be himself. I am a blank slate as it relates to this new Boykin baby, but a blank slate that is ready to be filled up because I realized I am ready to love again.

Tucker, it is forty-eight weeks. Tucker, I still miss you and will always remember you and your isms. Nubby-Bean, I met your mama. She jumped right up on my lap and looked at me with those yellow Boykin eyes. I told her that I loved you for your whole life and that you were the very best boy. She schnozzled me. The books are ready, Nubby-Bean. The website is coming live this weekend (sheilacoopermanbooks.com). Dex and Bufie: say hi to them. How are Cricket and Piper? Oreo: okay? What about Tootsie Roll Buster? All of them are greatly missed. And Tucky, I will talk to our newbie all about you and tell him how good a boy you were, and I will show him all your favorite spots, okay? I love you more, you know?

Mama

WEEK 49

For your reading pleasure, here are a few factoids about the number forty-nine. Forty-nine is the square of seven. It is the smallest triple of three squares (one, twenty-five, forty-nine). Do not ask me what that means. I am an English teacher, not a math teacher. Forty-nine is the year the California Gold Rush began. It is the atomic number of indium. Do not ask me what that is. I am an English teacher, not a chemistry teacher. Forty-nine has significance in both Judaism and Islam. Do not ask me what the significance is. I am an English teacher, not a theologian. Forty-nine is part of the San Francisco football team, commonly referred to as the 49ers. Forty-nine is a spiral galaxy in the constellation Cetus. And forty-nine is also the number of weeks that have passed since Tucker's physical presence left.

We have been pretty busy getting ready to welcome our newbie in a little over a week, give or take a few days. I am both nervous and excited. I got a little jolt in my stomach when the Chewy boxes started arriving. Tucker's favorite toys were the Wubba bunnies. Either he was Pavlovian-trained and recognized the shape of the box when I carried it in, or he associated the rise in my voice when I said, "Ooooh, look what I have for you. Look what's here," but whatever it was, he would be standing there anxiously awaiting whatever came out of the box. He would take it and run into the other room and sit with his special Wubba bunny in his mouth and close his eyes. We called it his meditation bunny. I still like those Wubbas. I wonder what the newbie will do with it.

The treats have been purchased, and they, too, are arriving. Kim Orsini, a Boykin Nation member, crafted a beautiful urn. It was too small to hold Tucker's remains, so another one was created. But the first one is now home to the training treats that will be used for our newbie. Tucker's face on the urn will be watching his newbie brother.

Truth be told, as much as you all know how much I loved Nubby-Bean, there were two weaknesses. He did not know how to walk on a leash. Not his fault. We have a big yard, but he was strong, and we could not really go anywhere with him. So the newbie will get leash-trained. Tucker's happy-boy personality also made it hard for him to control his jumping. I didn't mind it. I liked when he jumped up on me when he saw me, but it wasn't good because it could knock elderly people and little people over. And we have both of those in our family. So, this little bundle-of-brown-joy will have to learn to greet people in a different way.

Life teaches you lessons. Little ones and big ones. It has taught me that loss is real and that in order to survive that loss, you have to go through the process. You have to go through it to get through it. It has taught me there are times when, no matter how many people are around who support you, sometimes you need to go it alone. It has taught me there are times when having many people around who support you is just what you need, and you could not do it if you were going it alone. It has taught me loss and grief go hand in hand, but so do loss and love, and grief and love. It has taught me, at least in my experience, that the levels of love and grief are not equivalent. I believe the level of grief is exponential to the level of love. You love greatly; you grieve to some unknown exponential number. Do not ask me to explain what the number is. I am an English teacher, not a math teacher. But I do know this. To all who have suffered a loss like this, you understand. To all who have not yet suffered from it, I am happy for you, but I hope when the time comes, my journey will help you. And to all of you who are in it now, know that it is a roller coaster. You leave the platform, but you can't actually see the ride. Like those big, fancy, new types of roller coasters, you can't see the drops and the turns and the twists and the parts that turn you upside down and leave you hanging with the blood rushing to your head. And just when you think you can't take it anymore, the ride continues. And such is grief. But at some point, a different point for all, you will make it back to the platform. You might feel a little nauseated from the ups and downs your stomach took over the ride. You might have a little headache as the equilibrium of your conflicting emotions tries to reset, but you will get to the platform.

The writing that has helped me process my loss has helped me get to the point of being able to love again. Every single person who has read my posts and reached out to me over the last forty-nine weeks has helped me heal. It is one of the reasons I keep writing. I have to pay it forward. Perhaps some of you out there will find solace and relief in reading more about my journey.

Perhaps some of you out there will find solace and relief in writing yourself. Please visit the website that is now live and look at the writing exercises. Try one. Let me know if what you see helps your journey. The site is sheilacoopermanbooks.com

Nubby-Bean, forty-nine weeks ago, you broke my heart, but you still occupy a very important part of it. The newbie is coming soon. I am not sure what we will name him, but I will let you know. Please tell Bufie and Dex they are getting overweight with all the treats they keep asking for in the books. Chelse—well, you know, just kiss her. Tell Oreo his dad misses him. Tell the other Oreo that I am going to see his mama this week. Cricket deserves a hug, and Tootsie Roll Buster does, too. Piper is not forgotten, nor is Phoebe. It's hot, Tucker; get in the water.

Love you more,

Mama

WEEK 50

All my posts have been meant to help those who grieve. At first, my writing was designed to help me because I was suffering so much when Tucker died, but I found that over the weeks, I was helping others. And to me, that became a blessing. It is not that I was happy that others were suffering, but I felt less alone and felt that I was surrounded by people who understood the stark, naked pain of loss. And that was crucial in my healing journey. When I started getting feedback from people thanking me for my words, I started posting on many different sites dealing with grief. I believe that in this harsh and cruel world we are currently living in, if I could provide a modicum of relief to just one person, it would be worth it. I may not be able to ease the pain for everyone in the world, but if I can ease the pain for just one person, I have changed their world.

I read many posts from people, all of whom were in different stages of their own journeys. I felt jealous of those who seemed to be more at peace than I was. I was envious of their positions, believing they were the exceptions and that I would never ever be able to reach that level of peace and acceptance. I felt mired in my desperation and sadness. I read as many books as I could on the grieving process, trying as hard as I could to understand the progression. I truly lived the words that people expressed. Grief is not linear. You can feel better one day, but then boom, feel stuck in your grief the next, and you just did not know when those ups and downs would occur.

The cancer diagnosis stung in many ways. So many people in my own world have suffered from cancer. My mom and my stepmom both died of cancer. Both died in their fifties. Hearing the cancer diagnosis for my Tucker opened those losses again. I started thinking about loss and grief and realized that grief is a human emotion that cannot be avoided. I was determined to work my way through the process. I looked at the many questions people posted. When will I know it is time? When am I going to feel better? Why did this happen? Why do I feel so guilty? What could I have done? Did I do anything wrong? I asked them all. Sometimes I did not really agree with the answers, especially when people said, "Don't worry. You will know." How would I know? But you know; I knew. When my Tucker was suffering from anxiety because he could not breathe easily in those last moments, when he did not seem to be calmed by my presence, when he could not settle down, when the extra oxygen did not help, I knew, we knew. We gave him a peaceful exit.

We did everything possible to make our boy's life a good life. We reveled in his happiness and his quirks. When Nubby-Bean got sick, we did everything to help. We played with him, we cooked special food for him, we loved him. We did nothing wrong. It was not our fault that he got cancer, and it is not your fault, either. To anyone who is reading these words, know that your love for your boy or girl is the best gift you can give. I have read many posts over the last fifty weeks that have said the good memories will outweigh the bad. In the beginning, I did not believe that. Any thought I had made me cry. Any picture I looked at made me cry. Tucker in the pool, Tucker holding his bunny, Tucker swimming, Tucker on my lap during Tucker-Time. I could not deal with it. But those words that were said about the good memories overtaking the bad are true. I can look at photos of his beautiful face, and I smile. I can look at my Nubby-Bean and be happy that he was in my life. So, for all of you reading this, it does happen. The grief is still there, but it is softer, and with that softness came the expansion of my heart. My heart is bigger. My heart is ready to love again. So, to all of you who are feeling suffocated and can't breathe because of the crushing weight of grief and despair on your chest, know that whether you jump into a new love or not, the grief will soften. You will always remember and never forget that soul dog, that heart dog, and the memories will begin to make you smile instead of making you collapse in a heap.

So now, it is time to bring in the newbie. Our newbie will be a different heart dog. Our newbie will be loved and become part of our FAMBILY—the word we used to describe our life with Nubby-Bean. Our Nubby and our Newbie. We will love him the way only we can love, with a full heart made richer by what our Tucker taught us. We will welcome all his quirks and take great joy out of the new memories we will make. The beauty of the memories we have with Tucker will enrich and enhance our love for our newbie. And our newbie's name is Cooper. Just like I had dozens of nicknames for my Tucker based on his personality and the things he did, so will I find some unique ones for my Cooper. For everyone out there facing and dealing with the sadness and fear of losing a dog, let me tell you, there is room in your heart for another if you want. I did not, at first. I was just too damn afraid of having to face the inevitability of grief that must come with love, but the need to give and receive that love won. And I am glad it did. Our Cooper will thrive in our love, and we will thrive in his.

Writing has helped me. I want anyone who thinks they want to try it to read my writing prompts on my website sheilacoopermanbooks.com. I post ideas that hopefully will help. The site is brand new and still under construction, but the writing might help you. Try it.

WEEK 51

In a way, we have two newbies in the family. My granddaughter was born in May 2024. She is very cute. She has a big smile, and she makes a very cute round mouth when she smiles. But I do not know her yet as a person. I know she likes to drink her bottle when she is hungry and she likes to sleep when she is tired, but I do not know what makes her "tick" yet. That comes with time. I am looking forward to knowing what she will be like and what she will like. I am looking forward to knowing what will make her happy and what she likes to do.

Our other newbie, as you know, is our new little Cooper. Last week, I talked about Tucker and how all his quirks and Tuckerisms are part of me now and part of the memories. I can say that in the first week with little Cooper, David called him Tucker approximately seven times. "Tucker" slipped out of my mouth about five. Was it muscle memory, like getting on a bicycle after thirty years and you just start riding? Was it something deeper? A throwback to the life that is no longer? I do not know the answer to that, but each time I caught myself saying "Tucker," it pinged a little with thoughts like "I remember Tucker doing that" or "Tucker never did that." So Tucker's presence is here as I live through this new puppyhood, which, at night, is tiring. But

Tucker's presence in my head is not bringing pain; it's more like bittersweet thoughts that revolve around missing him and wishing he was still here, but his presence in my mind did not stop me from being thrilled by his interest in the new world that Cooper is discovering.

So what is he discovering? He likes to jump up and try to grab the weeping willow tree branches that are hanging down in the yard. Watching him try to navigate the branches brought a smile. He has a way of just suddenly plopping his body down into the tall grass in the yard. Immediately into the Boykin sprawl. He is a tiny puppy hidden in large grass, and the only way you know he is there is because that wagging nub is moving the grass. He will grow and that piece-of-cute will be replaced by something else that is cute.

Cooper is very active. He seems to be the ADHD version of a dog. He gets distracted very easily, but everything that distracts him is filled with joy. The toys, the sticks in the yard (that I do not encourage for digestion purposes), the tug-of-war ropes, the chair bottoms (definitely not encouraged), shoes (again not encouraged), and his bunnies that are bigger than him. We are still learning what his quirks are. I do know he likes to sit under my desk (as he is doing right now) when I work. I am looking forward to getting to know the others. Tucker did not like big black plastic bags, and he did not like when the sneeze monster hit David.

Hopefully, we will have lots of time to learn and lots of memories to make. We tried to put him in the pool yesterday, but that did not go over too well. Wait, a Boykin who does not gravitate to the water. It might just be too early. He wants to be near us all the time. He wants to exercise his little puppy teeth on everything, including my ankles, which is annoying. I am trying to figure out the best way to stop that. Any suggestions?

Cooper is a pup learning about life. Everything is new and exciting. We are a new family. David, me, Cooper. We will grow and learn together. Like my moms, who are no longer here but remain with me, so will Tucker. I will take what I learned from Tucker and direct all the love I have to welcome our new Cooper, Cooper Coopertin, Cooper Copernicus, La Cooperacha, Button, and Mischievous Mike into our home. The nicknames are coming.

To all of you who are grieving and who are suffering, know I am there with you. I know the pain and the heartbreak. The feelings of despair and isolation. The many questions you have and the guilt you might be experiencing. Know that you will wake up—one day—and realize that your unbearable pain will be lessened. It doesn't go away, but it is not as crippling.

Nubby-Bean, take a look at the website and let me know what to add. Please tell the Chelse that she has a very cute human baby sister now and that Tootsie Roll Buster is really being missed. Make sure Bufie and Dex are exercising and getting treats. Piper, Bodhi, Phoebe, Cricket, and Oreo are always in our thoughts.

Yes, I know, but I love you more.

WEEK 52

It is almost unbelievable to me that I am sitting here crafting this piece. Never in a million YEARS did I think that I would be religiously crafting writing about my Tucker each week on the anniversary of his passing, consistently for one year. Yes, one year. If anyone out there has been consistently reading my posts for the last fifty-two weeks, 365 days, one year, a complete revolution around the sun, then I am grateful. One year ago, I did not think I would be able to live one more day—never mind 365 days. One year ago, when my heart was ripped out of my chest and torn to shreds in front of me, I wished that I could have been the Tin Man from *The Wizard of Oz*. To have a heart was to experience pain and torture like I had never felt before. But to have a heart also means there was love. I read something that said, "Between the first hello and the last goodbye, there was love, so much love." I can't credit who said that, but it is very true. I want to talk a little bit about the period of a year.

In the Jewish faith, when you bury a loved one, you do not erect a monument when the person is interred. One year later, people gather around the gravesite for what is known as an unveiling. It is at this point that the monument that has been erected is revealed. The stone is covered by a cloth, and after a ceremony, the veil is lifted and the stone is unveiled. Why is this done? The year between the burial and the unveiling allows the mourners to come to terms with their loss and their grief. The year allows the initial shock and grief to subside and allows people to reflect and come to understand their relationship with the deceased. The act of unveiling the stone is a physical marker of the deceased person's final resting place. It serves as a way to honor his or her life. It is a place to visit that will give anyone who grieves the ability to be alone with his or her thoughts for the rest of their lives.

The ceremony also symbolizes the unveiling of one's memories and the legacy of the person who has passed. It signifies the person's soul has ascended and is at peace. The unveiling ceremony is also meant to give the mourners a chance to review how their lives have changed over the year and to remind them that mortality is inescapable. In the spirit of the ceremony, it symbolizes that life should be lived to its fullest. Another cherished tradition is lighting a candle that burns for twenty-four hours. These candles are called Yahrzeit candles. It is a Yiddish word that means "year time." It marks the anniversary of a loved one's death. On this anniversary, I will be lighting the rainbow candle I have been saving for a year.

So as a reflection point, at this one-year mark of losing Tucker, I can unveil what I most cherish about him and about life. I learned about life's simplicity from Tucker. His joy in a simple blue ball, a bone, happiness when someone he loved walked in, a nap. I really did come to understand life's simplest pleasures. A good cup of coffee with my husband. Watching my father enjoy a lobster, a great passage in a book, the beautiful view from the deck overlooking the backyard where Tucker loved to run. His very own "back forty."

Tucker showed me what unconditional love is. What it means to love without placing value judgments on anyone. What it means to love someone for who he or she is, not what he or she possesses or can give you. Tucker did not care what I was wearing or if we had the biggest house on the street or bought the most expensive things. Tucker loved us for the safety and security we gave him. That is the most important lesson. Feeling love, feeling safe, feeling secure with those you love.

When Tucker left his mama, she let him go. Her job was done. In whatever way canine moms separate from their offspring, she let him go to learn how to navigate his world and life. And that life was wonderful until the moment he left us. He has taught me to do the same with my children. I learned that having adult children means letting them go and not holding them back. Letting them go and allowing them to learn as they navigate growing into parenthood and respecting their decisions as they choose how to raise their families. Advise only when asked. Be a good listener. Make them realize they are loved no matter how old they are. I want to let them know I set them free to live their own lives, but they can always come home to eat. When we picked up our newbie, Cooper, I was surrounded by many Boykins. I had not been around Boykins in a year. And as I smiled and touched all of them, it was Tucker's mama that jumped on my lap. Mama to mama. I told her that Tucker was the bestest boy ever.

On this one-year angelversary, I can smile when I think of him. I can smile when I remember how he chased his balls and shied away from big black garbage bags. I remember with fondness our "Happy Times," the moments when Tucker would jump up into bed and squiggle between the two of us, his head on a pillow and his nub wagging. I can smile when I remember how he whined when his ball rolled under the couch and he couldn't get it. It was a sad and pitiful sound, and I immediately stopped whatever I was doing to help him. I smile when I remember how he knew what "high five" meant and how he would bark when we said, "Speak." I smile when I remember how my granddaughters used to say, "Tucker, dance," and he would stand up on his hind legs waiting for a treat. Yes, I have many fond memories of my Nubby-Bean, and I smile with each one.

One year later, I still miss him; I still wish he were here. I still feel that he was cheated out of some time on this planet, and to be honest, I was not ready for him to go. But his memory lives forever, and we have a new baby to love.

Tucker, on this day of your unveiling, I want you to know that love is forever. I want you to know that I have thought about you every single day, often more than once a day, for the past year, and to know that I will continue to do so for the rest of my life. I will give the best life I can to Cooper, and I hope you will be able to help him and guide him through puppyhood and life.

Say hi to Dex and Bufie. Oreo, Piper, Bodhi, and Phoebe are all missed. Cricket, who was taken way too soon, is also missed. Tootsie Roll Buster, your family still talks about you. And of course, the Chelse needs loving.

Nubby-Bean, I know you do too, but I love you more.

Mama

EPILOGUE

As I write this, I continue to write weekly about grief, healing, and the road to recovery. This book has chronicled my journey for fifty-two weeks. But if my grief journey is still ongoing, why am I stopping at fifty-two weeks? It is not a random decision, but a planned one because of the significance that fifty-two weeks, or one year, has.

Sociologists, psychologists, and grief counselors all discuss the importance of waiting a year before making any major life decisions. People experience a myriad of emotions after a loss. Depression is common. People have a difficult time simply dealing with daily activities of life while they are mourning their loss. The inability to think clearly, the self-doubt, the despair, the inattention. All these things can cloud a person's thinking and have deleterious effects on the decision-making process.

Grief, which seems to take center stage after a loss, is relentless and all-consuming. It can stop you in your tracks, and activities that were once rote and commonplace become insurmountable tasks. Mourning and loss can suddenly cause people to think about their purpose. Questions about one's own sense of identity develop. Wondering who you are becomes a nagging question since you feel part of you died along with the one you are mourning. All these conflicting feelings need to be sorted out. And in order to do so, you need time, and you must be able to accept the loss. That does not happen overnight.

Fifty-two weeks is also significant in the Jewish faith. When loved ones are interred, no headstone is installed. The headstone is usually revealed one year past death at a ceremony called an unveiling. The year between the death and the unveiling allows the grievers to experience a large variety of "firsts" without the lost loved one: the first birthday, the first holiday season, and so many more. The act of unveiling a headstone is symbolic. It represents a mourner's acceptance of the loss. It also represents the "unveiling" of memories and legacies. There has been a year to process the loss, a year to reflect on the importance the lost loved one had on your life, and a year to begin to realize that while life goes on, it goes on differently, and hopefully, one grows stronger having had the love you lost.

My grief journey has been personal, and I have chosen to share it with all who choose to read about it. Hopefully, it will help others who are grieving to know that healing takes time but does happen. The old adage that time heals all wounds is true. It also leaves some scars, and that's okay.

ABOUT THE AUTHOR

Dr. Sheila Cooperman is a retired English Language Arts teacher with a PhD in Literacy. She is the author of *The Rainbow Brigade*, a children's book series that addresses difficult topics such as dealing with a new baby sibling, a best friend moving away, or the loss of a parent. Through the power of words and books, Sheila aims to help others manage grief and adversity.

www.sheilacoopermanbooks.com

www.ingramcontent.com/pod-product-compliance
Lightning Source LLC
Chambersburg PA
CBHW032101090426
42743CB00007B/202